STICKY
FINGERS

Sophie Maletsky

STICKY FINGERS

- DIY -
Duct Tape
PROJECTS

EASY TO PICK UP, HARD TO PUT DOWN

ZEST BOOKS

35 Stillman Street, Suite 121
San Francisco, CA 94107
www.zestbooks.net

Juvenile Nonfiction/Crafts & Hobbies
Library of Congress control number: 2013951197
ISBN: 978-1-936976-54-6

Cover design: Dagmar Trojanek and Theresa Currie
Interior design: Marissa Feind, with Dagmar Trojanek and Theresa Currie

Manufactured in China
SCP 10 9 8 7 6 5 4 3 2 1
4500461508

Connect with Zest!
zestbooks.net/blog
zestbooks.net/contests
twitter.com/zestbooks
facebook.com/zestbook
facebook.com/BookswithATwist
pinterest.com/zestbooks

This is dedicated to my Grammy Yocom, who taught me to learn through play and let me carve soap when I was three. And my Pop Yocom, who told the best stories . . . ever!

Acknowledgments

They say it takes a village to raise a child . . . well, apparently it also takes one to write a crafting book.

There are so many people that made this all possible—the first being all the folks at Zest Books, who ended up with sticky fingers themselves! To Hallie Warshaw, who decided to give us a chance, and to Ann Edwards, who guided us every step of the way. Ann, you "stuck" with us through it all—we never could have done this without you.

I want to thank Tapebrothers.com, who actually sponsored the contest that gave us the basic blueprint for writing this book. To all the folks who entered the contest and to our winners, thanks so much for your creativity and sharing your talents so readily.

To all the kids and adults who have attended my classes at libraries, schools, and private homes . . . you guys were the inspiration who made this possible! Thank you for letting me teach you, and in turn, teaching me more than I could ever learn on my own.

To photographer and friend Nano Visser, who helped to photograph all the new projects we created for the book. We all feel intense gratitude to you and "the girls"! You are, in a word, an angel, although "the girls" are the ones with the wings.

To all our amazing models—Michael Jensen, Sarah Jensen, Antonia Lawrence, Marianna Lawrence, Annette Molina, Grace Visser, Nora Visser, Maya Zakhour, Hanna Rumsey, and baby Umi the monkey. You made our creations pop!

To Jill Grossman, who believes in me and my crew so much that she makes us believe too. You give us the strength to carry on each day, and I will never have words enough to thank you for your support. To Angie, for giving up her living quarters; Melissa, for the brownies; Connor, for his antics; and Chase, for not making fun of his brother on camera.

To Molinita who kept our office and the party-planning business running while we were all off writing a book. You are our anchor! We'd be adrift without you!

To Simone Chavoor, who took on the daunting task of editing the crafting section for our website and built the foundation for our DIYs—only now do I realize how hard it is to turn pictures and ideas into understandable, descriptive words.

Most importantly, I need to thank my family. Mom and Dad, thanks for all your support . . . for letting Freda and I sit on your living room floor making thousands of "house points," for taking those early morning calls to talk me down from the ledge, and for always believing that your kids were special, even when we didn't deserve such thoughts. For my unbelievably talented sister, who not only has the ability to understand my hand motions, badly sketched blueprints, and overly long explanations, but has the talent to turn all that into these amazing works of beauty. Who has spent countless hours photographing, designing, and redesigning projects, and done so without complaint (as long as she is fed at 2 hour intervals).

And lastly, but most earnestly, my husband Scott . . . who handled and managed every detail of this process without ever cracking or getting grumpy. Who put in so many late night hours cataloging photos, correcting my descriptions, and making sure that Ann got everything she needed. You are the most amazing man in the world, and I do consider myself the luckiest person alive to be married to you!

CONTENTS

INTRODUCTION   8

CHAPTER 1
Tools of the Trade   **11**
What do I need to get started?   12

CHAPTER 2
Your Workstation   **17**

CHAPTER 3
The Basics   **23**
Basic Duct Tape Strips   24
   Fold-Over Strip   24
   Double-Folded Strip   25
   Super-Strong Strip   25
Sticky Strips   26
Easy Duct Tape Fabric   27
Standard Duct Tape Fabric   28
Tarp-backed Duct Tape Fabric   30
Felt-backed Duct Tape Fabric   31
Woven Duct Tape Fabric   32
Clear Window   34
Basic Pouch   35
Basic Pouch with Flap   36
Magnet Closure   38
Single-Tongue Closure   39

Double-Tongue Closure   40
Button Closure   42
Ziploc Closure   44
Zipper Closure   46
Velcro Closure   47

CHAPTER 4
Quick Crafts   **49**
Tassel   50
Bow   52
Gift Bow   55
Fan-Fold Bow   58
Rosette   60
Layered Flower   64
Carnation   66
Rose Petal Flower   70
Leaf   73
Basic Sticker   74
Layered Sticker   76
Ruffle   78

CHAPTER 5
Wallets   **81**
Basic Wallet with Two Pockets   82
Simple Clutch Wallet   86
Multipocket Wallet   90
Advanced Clutch Wallet   94
Trifold Wallet with ID Holder   98
Checkbook Keeper   101

CHAPTER 6
Purses, Bags, and Cases   **105**
Watermelon Purse   106
Cupcake Purse   110
Makeup Case   114
Sunglasses Case   116
Checkerboard Beach Bag   119

Money Keeper 122
Smartphone Case 126
Tablet Case 130
Messenger Bag 134

CHAPTER 7
Wearable Duct Tape **139**
Support-Your-Cause Pin 140
Lanyard 142
Headband 145
Beads 148
Beaded Bracelet 150
Layered Jewelry 152
Simple Ring 155
Spike-Rose Ring 158
Spike Bracelet 160
King's Crown Spike Bracelet 163
Double-Spike Bracelet 166
Bits-and-Snips Bracelet 168
Choker 170
Tie 174
Belt 178

CHAPTER 8
At School **181**
Bookmark with Tassel 182
Luggage Tag 184
Locker Organizer 187

Pencil Case 190
Folder with Pockets 193
Altoid Tin First-Aid Kit 196
Book Cover 198
Lunch Bag 201
Backpack 204

CHAPTER 9
In Your Room **209**
Desk Organizer 210
Dry-Erase Board 212
Checkerboard 215
Woven Basket 218
Picture Frame 220
Jewelry Stand 224
Earring Tree 227

CHAPTER 10
Every Last Bit of the Roll **231**
Using the End Tape 232
Using the Center if the Roll 234

Conclusion **235**
Templates **236**
Index **238**
About the author **240**

INTRODUCTION

It used to be that duct tape came in only one color: silver. Mind you, this was not a pretty, shiny silver; rather, it was a dull sort of battleship gray. Back then, duct tape wasn't a very exciting craft material at all, but people did appreciate some of its other amazing qualities: The tape was superstrong, supermalleable, and supersticky. You could basically use it to hold any two objects together. People used to say, "If it moves and it shouldn't, then duct tape it."

Throughout my years as a party planner specializing in craft projects, I first witnessed, then joined, a duct tape revolution. It began slowly and simply with just a few colors—black, white, and red. Then blue, yellow, and orange made an appearance. Within a year, there were neon colors like hot pink and antifreeze chartreuse. As more and more people began to use it for more and more projects, the crafting world began to take notice. It wasn't long before one could find more than fifteen colors at the craft store in hues ranging from baby pink to aquamarine. Then came patterned duct tape, and soon everything from flames to flying pigs was claiming shelf space in stores.

What makes people go so crazy over duct tape? The answer is simply this: You can make or decorate virtually anything with it! It's sticky and has the consistency of fabric, which means you can make everything from purses to clothing out of it. Plus, now that duct tape comes in almost every color and pattern imaginable, you can use it to create something that's uniquely you.

I've been fortunate enough to work with many creative duct tape crafters and develop tons of fun and unique duct tape projects. Many of the projects included in this book are inspired by these creative crafters and the ways they've developed and adapted their own duct tape projects. You'll see some of these projects called out with "Sticky High-Fives" to the crafters who developed or inspired them.

I've also had the opportunity to bring this material to the masses, both through my face-to-face events and on my YouTube channel. My goal with duct tape crafting is simple: Pass on the skills, techniques, tricks, and tips that I've learned so that crafters everywhere can master this amazing material. The great thing about duct tape is that once you have a basic understanding of how pieces go together, you can expand on those basic patterns and create virtually anything!

I hope that you'll find this book to be an inspiration and will let it guide you into the world of the duct. Have fun, and remember: You're limited only by your imagination—and by the amount of tape on your roll!

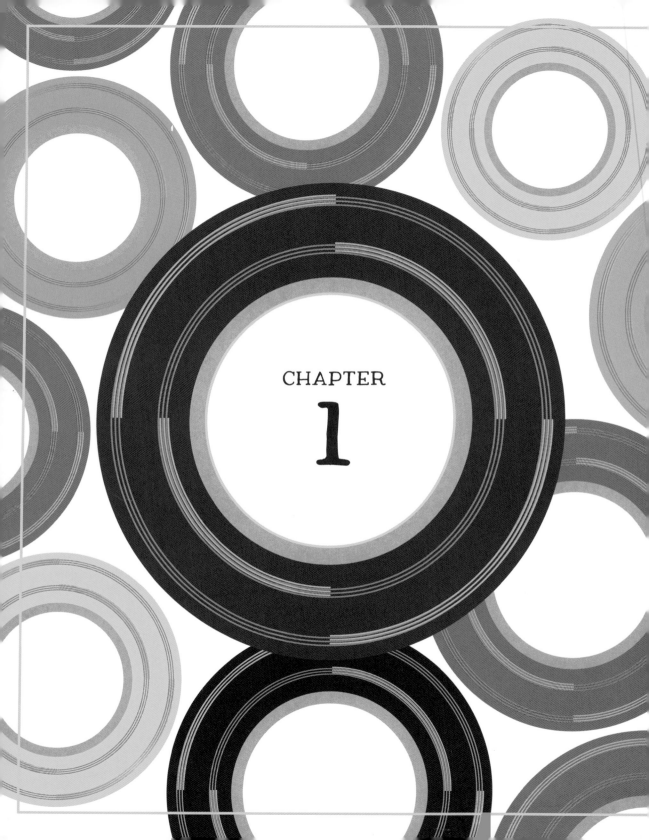

CHAPTER

1

TOOLS OF THE TRADE

It doesn't take much to start crafting with duct tape—just a few tools, some tape, and a little bit of space! In Chapter 1, you'll get a rundown of what you need and where to get it, plus tips on recommended brands and all the different types of tape. It's important to learn all about the tools of the trade before you start ripping, snipping, and taping. Take a quick look through this chapter and you'll be ready to go in no time.

Crafting with duct tape can take a little more time and patience than some other kinds of crafting, like braiding friendship bracelets or doing a paint-by-number project. Mastering the essential skills and methods of duct tape crafting can take some effort, but once you've got the basics down and have a feel for the materials, you can create or embellish almost anything—seriously, anything, from clothes to jewelry to bags to furniture. The only limit is your imagination.

What Do I Need to Get Started?
You really need only three things to start your taping adventure:
1. A work surface
2. A roll of duct tape
3. A good pair of nonstick scissors

Work Surfaces
Your work surface might be the single most important crafting item other than the duct tape itself. Duct tape is made with very strong glue, which can easily stick to and even damage almost any surface you use it on. You don't want to put a lot of time and effort into a duct tape project, only to pull it up from your work surface and realize you've taken a layer of varnish off your family's dining room table.

You want your work surface to be flat, smooth, and sturdy. The tape should stick, but not bond, to the surface. Test any work surface you plan to use with a tiny strip of tape before you start a project.

Many crafters are fans of the self-healing cutting mat. These mats were initially designed for sewing, but they're ideal for duct tape crafting because they're flexible and sturdy, and you can cut right on them with an X-acto knife. Plus, most mats come printed with a measuring grid right on the surface, so it's easy to line up strips of duct tape.

Another option is to make your own portable work surface. Simply wrap a piece of canvas or cotton fabric around a sturdy, thin piece of wood and staple the fabric in place. You can't cut with an X-acto knife on the fabric, but otherwise it's a great work surface. You can even take it on road trips or to a friend's house or stick it in your backpack to use during your lunch break.

Where Can I Buy Duct Tape?

These days, you can find duct tape almost anywhere. You should be able to find colored and patterned tapes at hardware and home-improvement stores, big-box stores like Target and Walmart, and arts-and-crafts stores like Michaels, Hobby Lobby, A.C. Moore, and JoAnn Fabrics. Some dollar stores even carry duct tape now. DuctTapeBrothers.com and Amazon.com both offer a huge array of tapes to online shopers.

Brand Breakdown

Here are some of the pros and cons of the most common brands of duct tape:

3M: This duct tape is superstrong, superdurable, and rips well, and you get a lot on the roll. The only drawback is that it comes only in black, white, and red.

Alex: This duct tape is usually sold in crafting kits. The tape colors tend to be muted.

Duck (basic colors): This is the tape that started the revolution! Basic colors come in 20-yard rolls. The tape rips cleanly and is supersticky, making it a good standard tape for most projects.

Duck (patterns): Duck brand makes an amazing variety of patterned duct tape. Be warned: The rolls of patterned tape cost the same as or more than basic color rolls and contain only half as much tape.

Work-Surface Do's and Don'ts

NEVER USE:	OKAY TO USE:
Cardboard	Clipboard
Brick or stone	Cookie sheet covered with a tight-fitting T-shirt
Cork or foam	
Painted concrete, wood, or metal	Fabric tablecloth
	Marble counter
Paper tablecloth	Plastic table
Plastic tablecloth	Porcelain-tile counter
Varnished furniture	Self-healing plastic cutting mat
	Unfinished wood
	Very low-pile carpet

Scotch: This duct tape is thinner and a bit more transparent than Duck brand tape. It doesn't rip as easily and has a plastic quality to it, but it costs less than Duck brand does.

Tape Brothers: This economical duct tape works well and comes in 60-yard rolls, but it comes only in colors, not in patterns.

U-Line: This is another economical tape that comes in 60-yard rolls. It also comes only in colors, not in patterns.

Other Tapes That You Can Use with Duct Tape

Hockey stick tape: This is a very thin, fabric-based tape that's best used for embellishing your projects. It's both durable and flexible.

Mylar tape: This tape is supershiny, but it's very thin and should be used only for embellishing your projects.

Packing tape: Although this isn't a great tape for every project, it makes a really great window for an ID pocket (see page 95) and a surface for a dry-erase board (see page 212).

Spike tape: This tape is used primarily for theater, but it comes in 1/4-inch-wide, 1/2-inch-wide, and 1-inch-wide rolls, which makes it perfect for embellishing your projects. It comes in neon as well as in standard colors.

Tapes to Avoid Using

Electrical tape: Although it comes in some great colors, electrical tape peels right off and shouldn't be used for duct tape projects.

Masking tape: Although it comes in a variety of colors, this tape isn't very flexible. This is a great tape to use with paper or cardboard instead of duct tape.

Standard Scotch tape: This tape is too brittle to use for duct tape projects.

Washi tape: Washi tape comes in great colors and patterns, but it isn't sticky enough for duct tape projects. Washi tape should be used only on paper.

How Much Tape Do I Need to Get Started?

A good starter set of duct tape is two rolls of colored tape and one roll of patterned tape. One standard 20-yard roll of colored duct tape will make between three and four purses or about seven wallets. Once you have some duct tape projects under your belt, you can start planning your projects and your tape needs accordingly.

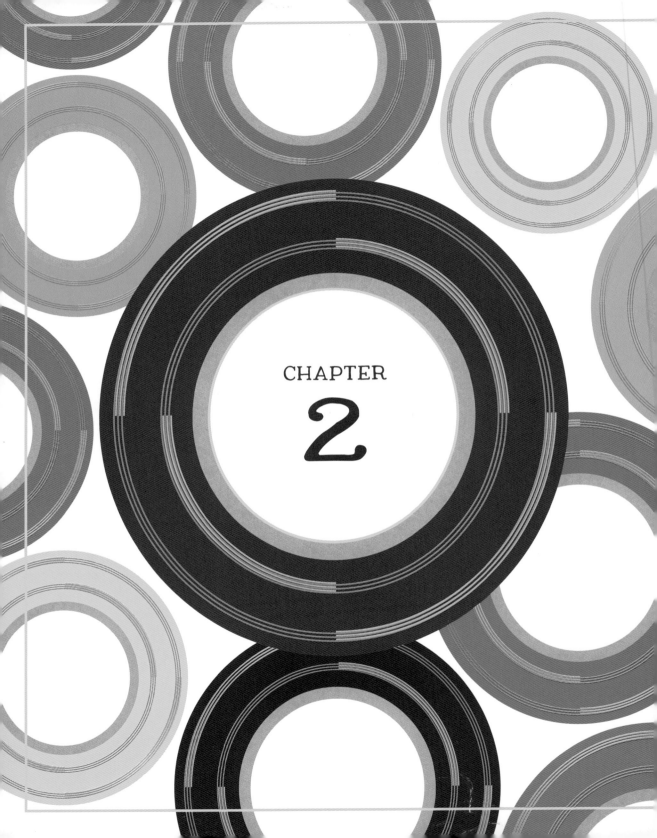

CHAPTER

2

YOUR WORKSTATION

Now that you have all the basic tools and supplies you need to make pretty much any duct tape craft imaginable, where are you going to put them? Chapter 2 will show you how to create the ideal workstation for your crafting style. Your workstation can be as elaborate or as simple as you like, so adapt it to fit your needs and take it with you wherever you go!

In an ideal world, every duct tape crafter would have the dream workstation: room to organize their tape, ample light for cutting and sticking, an abundance of workspace, and an organized bin of embellishments, notions, and tools.

The reality is, you probably have to make do with a corner of your room, or with moving your supplies on and off the kitchen table mid project. Luckily, it's pretty easy to make a portable workstation out of things you probably already have around the house, which will help keep all your materials organized, neat, and accessible.

To make your portable workstation, start with a clear plastic storage bin, like the ones you use to store sweaters and blankets under the bed. A shallow box about 6 ½ inches high will be tall enough to hold the rolls of duct tape on their sides, but flat enough to fit under most beds. You can also use a deeper bin, depending on your needs. It's okay to use a colored bin, but the clear plastic will ensure that you can easily take an inventory of your tape and supplies at a glance.

Here are some tips for making your portable workstation work for you:

• Line the rolls of tape up side by side, categorized by color, pattern, or in order of most-used to least-used. Keeping the rolls aligned will help you grab what you need quickly, and keep track of what you're running low on.

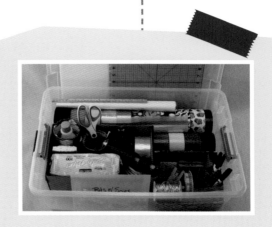

• Use a small box to store the small crafting supplies, like magnets and sticky-backed Velcro. You can buy an inexpensive notion box at a hardware or craft store, or make one using a shoebox or tea box. If you make your own notion box, use other small boxes, like soap, pasta, or cereal boxes, to make compartments inside of it. Toilet paper tubes make perfect dividers for smaller items like ribbon and elastic scraps.

• If your box is tall enough, glue the cardboard centers from used-up duct tape rolls together to make scissor and pen holders. See the Desk Organizer on page 210 for other ways to use these cardboard centers.

• Don't worry about gathering all the supplies you need and filling up your portable workstation before you start crafting. Build your box over time, and add pieces as you master different techniques and projects.

Must-Haves	The Next Level
Duct tape	Clear packing tape
Scissors	Dry-erase marker
Work surface	Envelopes for storing bits and scraps, inspirational images, and patterns
	Hole punch
	Nail polish remover or baby wipes for cleaning scissors
	Parchment paper
	Ruler or tape measure
	Scouring or scrub sponge for cleaning scissors
	Tarp
	X-acto knife

Everything but the Kitchen Sink

Barrettes or clips

Beads

Buttons

D-rings

Dog clips

Earring hooks and backs

Elastic

Embellishment tapes

Felt

Glue gun

Jewels and other
  embellishments

Key rings

Magnets

Paper clips

Permanent markers

Pipe cleaners

Ribbon

Sticky-backed magnets

Sticky-backed Velcro

Twist ties

Wire brads

Ziploc bags

Zippers

CHAPTER

3

THE BASICS

When you look at a completed duct tape project, it can be hard to imagine that once it was just a roll of duct tape. But here's a secret: Most duct tape crafts are just variations on a few basic techniques. In Chapter 3, you'll learn how to make the basic elements of most projects, including duct tape fabric, closures, and a basic pouch. These techniques will become very useful for the more complex projects in later chapters, but they are also essential building blocks for original projects as well. This is where your duct tape education really begins . . .

Basic Duct Tape Strips

LEVEL: ●○○○○ ⫶ **TIME:** Less than 5 minutes

MATERIALS

Scissors

Duct tape

Ruler

Duct tape strips are an essential part of a variety of projects, from belts to bracelets, rings, closures, loops, and more. This technique works best for making strips up to 12 inches in length, but if you need a longer strip, simply attach multiple strips together.

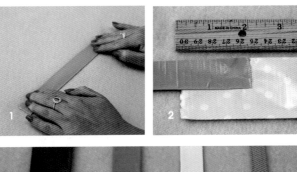

Fold-Over Strip

1 Cut a strip of duct tape up to 12 inches long and lay it sticky side up on the work surface. Fold the bottom edge of the tape up to the top edge lengthwise and smooth out any bubbles or creases with your fingers.

2 To make the strip longer than 12 inches, lay a second piece of tape down, sticky side up, and place the finished strip on it, with about 2 inches overlapping at the short end and the top long edges of the tapes aligned. Fold the sticky tape up to seal the strip like you did in step 1. Repeat these steps until the fold-over strip is the desired length.

3 You can make the fold-over strip as thin as you want. Simply trim the fold-over strip to the desired width.

Double-Folded Strip

1 Cut a strip of duct tape to the desired length and place it sticky side up on the work surface. Fold the bottom edge lengthwise half way up the sticky side of the tape.

2 Next, fold the sealed part of the strip up and over itself onto the remaining sticky bit of tape to make a $^3/_4$-inch-wide sealed strip.

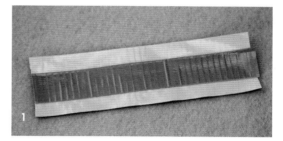

Super-Strong Strip

1 Make a fold-over strip (facing page) the desired length. Next, lay another piece of duct tape the same length as the finished strip on the work surface, sticky side up. Place the fold-over strip in the middle of the sticky tape.

2 Fold the bottom edge of the sticky tape lengthwise up and over the completed strip, and then fold the top edge of the sticky tape down over the completed strip to seal the super-strong strip.

3-FOLD AND 4-FOLD STRIPS

3-FOLD STRIP
To make a 3-fold strip, fold lengthwise one-third of the way up the sticky side of the tape. Then, continue folding that sealed part up and over itself two more times until you reach the top edge of the tape, making a $^1/_2$-inch strip.

4-FOLD STRIP
To make a 4-fold strip, fold lengthwise one-quarter of the way up the sticky side of the tape. Then, continue folding that sealed part up and over itself three more times until you reach the top edge of the tape, making a $^1/_4$-inch strip.

Sticky Strips

LEVEL: ●○○○○ ┊ TIME: Less than 5 minutes

MATERIALS

Scissors

Duct tape

Ruler

A sticky strip is a piece of duct tape fabric with ¹/4 inch of sticky tape along an edge. These sticky strips are important parts of projects like the Multipocket Wallet (page 90) and the Beads (page 148), so turn back to this section any time you need to use this technique. You can use different-colored tapes for each side of the strip or the same colors if you want the strip to look like one piece of fabric.

One-Inch Strip

Cut a strip of duct tape to the desired length and lay it on the work surface, sticky side up. Fold the bottom edge of the tape up lengthwise on the sticky side, leaving about ¹/4 inch of sticky tape showing.

Alternatively, you can make a 2-inch wide sticky strip by folding the short end of the tape up, instead of folding along the long side.

Two-Inch Strip

Cut a strip of duct tape to the desired length and lay it on the work surface, sticky side up. Place a second piece of tape the same length on top of the first piece, sticky side to sticky side, leaving about ¹/4 inch of the bottom piece's sticky edge showing. Fold one of the long sticky sides up so that only one sticky strip is visible.

Easy Duct Tape Fabric

LEVEL: ●●○○○ ¦ TIME: 10 minutes

MATERIALS

Scissors

Duct tape

Duct tape fabric is the starting point for nearly every duct tape project. You can make simple, solid-color duct tape fabric or create wacky designs by using different colors and patterns of duct tape. There's more than one way to make duct tape fabric, so see pages 28–33 for other versions of this project staple.

1 Cut a strip of duct tape to the desired length and lay it on the work surface, sticky side up. Place a second strip of tape on top of it, ¹/4 inch from the top, sticky sides together.

2 Flip the strips of tape over and place a third strip of tape, sticky side down, overlapping the bottom edge of the fabric side of the tape by about ¹/4 inch. Repeat until the fabric is the desired length.

3 Fold the sticky ends over on the top and bottom edges of the fabric to seal.

4 Trim the ragged side edges of the fabric so they are clean, with no sticky tape showing.

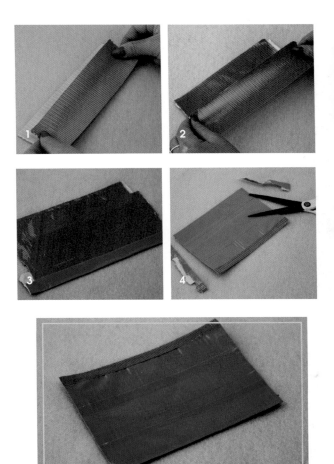

Standard Duct Tape Fabric

LEVEL: ●●○○○ ┊ TIME: 10 minutes

MATERIALS

Scissors

Duct tape

Standard duct tape fabric is stronger than easy duct tape fabric but still flexible enough to use for nearly every duct tape project. You can make a lot of duct tape fabric at once and save it for future projects or make fabric as you go in the patterns and colors you like best.

1 Cut a strip of duct tape the desired length and lay it sticky side down on the work surface. Smooth the tape out with your fingers so that there are no air bubbles or creases.

2 Unroll another strip of tape the same length as the first one and stick the long sides of the 2 pieces together, overlapping them slightly by about ¼ inch. Smooth the tape out with your fingers to remove any air bubbles or creases and to ensure it's stuck firmly to the first strip.

3 Continue laying down overlapping strips of tape until you reach the desired fabric size.

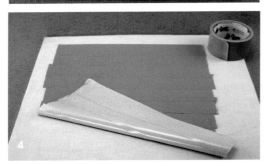

4 Starting from the outside edge of the first strip you stuck down, carefully peel the sheet up and away from the work surface.

5 Flip the entire sheet over so that it's sticky side up. Now you'll cover the sticky side of the fabric with tape. Starting at the edge of the fabric, lay down strips of duct tape, sticky sides together and perpendicular to the first strips to help hold the fabric together.

6 Continue laying down strips, slightly overlapping as in step 2, until you reach the end of the fabric. You can alternate tapes to create a pattern or add more color, if you like.

7 Trim the edges of the fabric to get rid of any sticky, jagged bits.

Tarp-backed Duct Tape Fabric

LEVEL: ●●○○○ ┊ TIME: 15 minutes

MATERIALS

Scissors
Ruler (optional)
Tarp
Duct tape

Duct tape is expensive, and some large projects require a lot of duct tape fabric. In those cases, tarp-backed duct tape fabric is a great way to stretch your duct tape dollars. With little more than a tarp and some duct tape, you're on your way to creating everything from backpacks and bags to duct tape clothing.

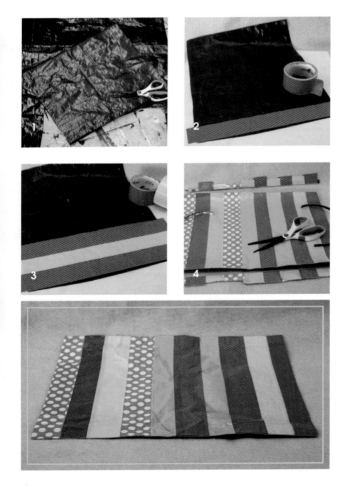

1 Cut a piece of tarp slightly larger than the size you need for the project.

2 Cut a strip of duct tape a little longer than the length or width of the tarp (depending on which way you want the stripes oriented) and place it sticky side down on the tarp. Smooth out the tape with your fingers so that there are no air bubbles or creases.

3 Continue laying down overlapping strips of tape on the tarp, with the long sides of the tape overlapping each other by about 1/4 inch.

4 Trim the edges of the fabric to get rid of any sticky, jagged bits. Cutting both the tape and the tarp will help seal the two together.

Felt-backed Duct Tape Fabric

LEVEL: ● ● ○ ○ ○ ⋮ **TIME:** 15 minutes

MATERIALS

Scissors

Felt

Ruler (optional)

Duct tape

For more delicate projects like the Smartphone Case (page 126) or the Sunglasses Case (page 116), felt-backed duct tape fabric is a good choice. Things like sunglasses and smartphones scratch easily and need a bit more protection than standard duct tape fabric can provide. The soft felt protects your items, doesn't fray, and doesn't shed.

1 Cut a piece of felt the size you need for the project.

2 Lay the felt flat on the work surface and begin covering it with strips of duct tape, like you did for the tarp-backed duct tape fabric (facing page), but making sure the tape extends beyond the edge of the felt by about 1 inch on all sides.

3 Once you've covered one side of the felt entirely with strips of duct tape, take two long strips of tape and stick them along the ragged long edges, leaving about half of the width of the tape overhanging.

4 Flip the fabric over so that the felt side is facing up. Fold the long edges down and stick the tape to the felt. Fold the short edges down and stick the tape to the felt, making those long edges clean and uniform. You'll see that two ends will need to be secured with a small strip of extra tape.

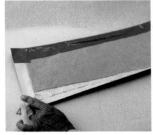

Woven Duct Tape Fabric

LEVEL: ●●●○○ | TIME: 20 minutes

MATERIALS

Fold-Over Strips
(page 24)

Scissors

Duct tape

Ruler

Using woven duct tape fabric for a project is one way to add something special to a simple design. The checkerboard pattern adds color and flair, and the woven fabric is strong and durable. Try substituting woven fabric for standard duct tape fabric on your favorite project and see what you come up with!

1 To create the weaving strips, cut fold-over strips to the desired length. Trim the sides of the strips if necessary.

2 Create a border strip by cutting a piece of tape to the desired width of the fabric. Fold this strip in half lengthwise with the sticky side facing out.

3 Take the first set of strips and lay their ends next to each other on top of the sticky border tape. The fold of the border strip should be on top, and the open edge should be on the bottom. Next, take one of the other strips and weave it over and under the hanging strips. (In the photo, this is the green strip.) Push the long edge of the horizontal weaving strip up so it's touching the border strip with no gaps between.

HOW MANY STRIPS

Remember: The border pieces of tape will add 1 inch to each side of the duct tape fabric. So, if you want to make a 6-by-8-inch piece of fabric, you'll need four 8-inch fold-over strips and six 6-inch fold-over strips.

4 Take the second horizontal strip and weave it through the hanging strips the opposite way you wove the first strip. You will see a checkerboard pattern start to form. Push the long edge of this horizontal strip up to meet the edge of the first horizontal strip with no gaps between.

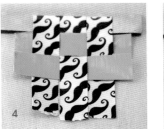

5 Continue weaving horizontal strips in this pattern until you reach the end of the hanging strips.

6 Carefully peel the sticky side of the border strip up from the work surface. Fold the border strip over the tops of the hanging strips to secure them in place. Measure and cut 3 more strips of duct tape to use as the borders on the other three sides of the fabric.

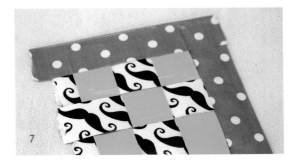

7 Stick one of the border pieces of tape along another open edge of the fabric, lining up the corner and half of the width, and fold it over on itself, sealing in that edge of the fabric. Repeat for the other two sides to finish the piece of fabric.

Clear Window

LEVEL: ●●○○○ ┊ TIME: 5 minutes

MATERIALS

Clear packing tape
Duct tape
Scissors

Packing tape is a cheap and widely available material you can use to make a window for an ID pocket or in another project. However, packing tape is thinner than duct tape, and it can be tricky to work with. Here's how to make a bubble-free window out of packing tape.

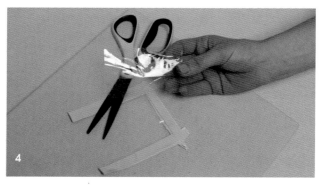

1 Place 2 strips of packing tape sticky side down on the work surface, overlapping by 1/4 inch as if you were making duct tape fabric. The strips of tape should be equal in length and twice as long as you want the window to be.

2 Cut 1/2-inch strips of duct tape to make a frame around the packing tape, also sticky side down. (The strips don't need to be perfect; you'll discard them later.)

3 Flip the window over and fold it in half, securing the duct tape ends to each other and smoothing out any bubbles or creases with your fingers. The duct tape should give you more control and help keep bubbles out of the packing tape.

4 Cut the packing tape square out of the duct tape frame. Now you have a clear window to use for any project.

Basic Pouch

LEVEL: ●●○○○ ┆ TIME: 20 minutes

MATERIALS

Easy Duct Tape Fabric (page 27)

Scissors

Duct tape

The pouch is the starter piece for everything from wallets to purses to basically anything else that holds your stuff. Use a simple pouch to store small items on your desk, like paper clips, or in your bathroom, like bobby pins.

1 Start with a piece of easy duct tape fabric that's twice as long as you want the finished pouch to be. For example, if you want a 6-inch-long pouch, the fabric should be 12 inches long. Fold the duct tape fabric in half into the shape you want the finished pouch to be.

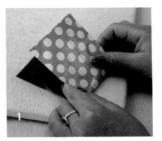 

2 Cut a strip of duct tape that is about 1 inch longer than the width of the pouch. Rip this strip in half lengthwise to make 2 strips.

3 Place the strips along the open sides of the folded duct tape pouch. About half of the strips should be on the fabric and half should be hanging over the edge. The ends of the strips will hang over the open top and folded bottom of the pouch, too.

 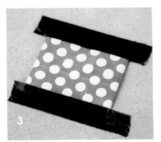

4 Flip the pouch over and seal both sides by folding over the sticky tape. You will have a little extra overhang that seals itself into 4 little tabs on either side of the edges. Trim off the little extra tabs with the scissors. To finish off the pouch, line the open edges with another strip of tape.

Basic Pouch with Flap

LEVEL: ● ● ○ ○ ○ ┊ **TIME:** 15 minutes

MATERIALS

Easy Duct Tape
Fabric (page 27)

Duct tape

Dry-erase marker

Scissors

The steps for this project are very similar to the steps for the Basic Pouch (page 35), except that this pouch has a closing flap to secure your items inside.

1 Start with a piece of duct tape fabric that is three times as long as you want the finished pouch to be. Fold up one-third of the duct tape fabric to begin making the pouch.

2 To finish the pouch, seal and trim the sides as directed for the basic pouch (page 35), but leave the top part of the fabric hanging end unsealed.

3 You can keep the closure flap the shape it is, or you can use a dry-erase marker to trace any shape you want on the duct tape fabric and cut it out to make a more ornate flap. Just make sure to leave at least 1 inch of straight fabric at the top folding part of the closure so the pouch will have a solid seal across the top. Wipe off any dry-erase marks after trimming the flap.

4 Choose your favorite closure, like a single-tongue closure or Velcro closure, and finish the pouch by attaching it (see pages 38–47 for closures).

Make a 3-D pouch

1 To make a pouch with a flat bottom, place your pointer finger inside one corner of the pouch. With the thumb and pointer finger of your other hand, pinch the corner of the pouch to make a triangle. Fold the triangle up onto the side of the pouch or down under the bottom of the pouch, depending on what look you prefer.

2 Use a strip of tape to secure the triangle to the side (or bottom) of the pouch. Repeat on the other side of the pouch.

Magnet Closure

LEVEL: ● ● ○ ○ ○ ┆ TIME: 5 minutes

MATERIALS

Basic Pouch with
Flap (page 36)

2 neodymium
magnets

Scissors

Duct tape

Magnet closures offer a simple and elegant way to keep purses, pouches, and wallets closed. The best type of magnet for these projects is called a neodymium, or "rare earth," magnet. These magnets are thin, small, and super strong. Note: Magnets can be dangerous, especially if ingested. Keep magnets away from very small children and pets.

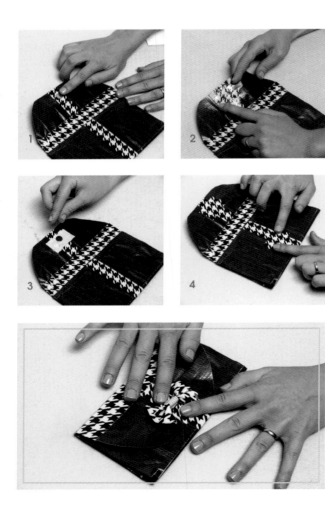

1 Open the flap of the pouch and place 1 magnet on the inside of the flap, centered and slightly in from the top edge.

2 Tape the magnet in place, making sure to match the tape color to the project to disguise the magnet. There should be at least 1/2 inch of tape around the magnet on all sides.

3 On top of the taped magnet, place another matching square of tape, sticky side up. Hold the second magnet over the sticky tape and drop it. The magnet will flip to its appropriate polarized side and stick to the other magnet through both layers of tape.

4 Fold the flap down so that the pouch is closed. Rub your fingers over the flap to seal the second magnet and tape into place. Reopen the flap and seal any open spots in the tape around both magnets.

Single-Tongue Closure

LEVEL: ● ● ● ○ ○ | **TIME:** 10 to 15 minutes

MATERIALS

Scissors

Fold-Over Strip twice as long as the length of the pouch (page 24)

Duct tape

Basic Pouch with Flap (page 36)

A single-tongue closure is a simple way to keep anything with a flap securely closed. It also adds a nice 3-D element to your project and gives you the chance to use other colors or patterns of duct tape for the closure pieces.

1 Cut the fold-over strip in half, then cut one half in half lengthwise to make 2 thin strips.

2 Tape the thicker duct tape strip directly onto the middle underside of the flap. This piece is the tongue part of the closure.

3 Close the flap and place 1 of the strips parallel to the bottom of the pouch, at least 1/2 inch below the bottom edge of the flap. Tape this strip in place on both sides, using small pieces of matching or complimentary duct tape, and making sure to leave enough space for the tongue to fit through the tab you're making.

4 You can trim the tongue into any shape, as long as it still fits through the closure tab. Slip the tongue through the tab to secure the flap of the pouch.

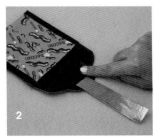

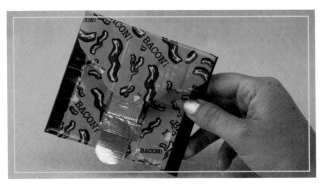

Double-Tongue Closure

LEVEL: ● ● ● ○ ○ ⦙ TIME: 10 to 15 minutes

MATERIALS

Scissors

Fold-Over Strip three times longer than the length of the pouch (page 24)

Duct tape

Basic Pouch with Flap (page 36)

The Double-Tongue Closure is even more secure than the Single-Tongue Closure (page 39). Use this closure when you really need to keep your stuff secure, like in a wallet or clutch.

1 Cut about one-third off the fold-over strip, then cut this piece in half lengthwise to make 2 thin strips.

2 Tape the thicker duct tape strip directly onto the middle underside of the flap. This piece is the tongue part of the closure.

A WRAPAROUND CLOSURE

To make a super-secure double lock, use a wraparound closure: Make the tongue extra long so that it can slip through the bottom lock, wrap around the back of the pouch, slip down through the top flap lock, and fit through the bottom lock a second time.

3 Close the flap and place one of the thin strips parallel to the bottom of the pouch, at least $^1/2$ inch below the bottom edge of the flap. Tape this strip in place on both sides, using small pieces of matching or complimentary duct tape, and making sure to leave enough space for the tongue to fit through the tab you're making.

4 Now, attach the second thin strip of tape centered on the outside of the flap, aligned with the first thin strip. The tongue closure should slide through both of these locking strips, so leave space for the tongue to fit under the top locking strip as you did with the first one.

5 Slip the tongue beneath the first locking strip, then fold it up and slip it under the second strip to lock it. Trim off any excess tongue leaving about an inch of tongue hanging over the end of the pouch.

Button Closure

LEVEL: ●●○○○ ⋮ **TIME:** Less than 5 minutes

MATERIALS

Twist tie or pipe cleaner

Button with at least 2 holes

Pouch or other project that needs a closure

X-acto knife or scissors

Dry-erase marker

Buttons are an effective method for keeping a pouch closed, and they're also a great way to add a 3-D bit of color to your project.

1 Slip one end of the twist tie or pipe cleaner up through one of the holes in the button. Bend the twist tie in half and feed it down through the front side of the second hole in the button.

2 Carefully make a small hole on the pouch where you would like to attach the button. To get the cleanest buttonhole cut, use an X-acto knife (use extreme caution), but a pair of scissors will work fine, too.

> **TIP!**
>
> **A MATCHING BUTTON**
> For a clean, uniform look, cover the button with duct tape in the same color or pattern as the pouch.

3 Slip both ends of the twist tie into the hole. Open the two ends like you would the ends of a brad and flatten them against the inside of pouch, pulling the button tight against the outside of the pouch. Secure the twist ties with a strip or two of duct tape.

4 Close the flap of the pouch over the button. With your fingers, feel through the pouch flap to find the top and bottom edges of the button, and mark them on the flap with a dry-erase marker.

5 Carefully use the X-acto knife or scissors to cut a slit between the dry-erase marks (use extreme caution). Wipe off the marks with your finger or a cloth. Slip the button through the hole you just cut.

Ziploc Closure

LEVEL: ● ● ● ○ ○ ⫶ TIME: 15 minutes

MATERIALS

Ziploc bag
Scissors
Duct tape
Permanent marker

Ziploc closures are handy because you can often find Ziploc bags right in your pantry, or at least at the grocery store. Ziploc closures are strong, and they lock the entire top of the pouch. They're great for the Lunch Bag (page 201), Basic Pouch (page 35), and Makeup Case (page 114).

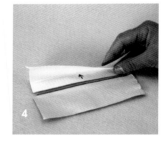

1 Seal the Ziploc bag and cut it off about ¼ to ½ inch below the closure. Discard the bag and trim the ends of the closure piece until it is ½ inch wider than the width of your project.

2 Slide the closure pieces apart and lay them on the work surface so that the ridged sides of both closures face up. Mark the top edges of both closure pieces with arrows pointing up, to ensure you don't accidentally flip the closures over.

3 Rip a strip of duct tape ¼ inch longer than the Ziploc closure and place it along the top edge of one of the closure pieces, close to the ridge without overlapping it. Repeat along the other side of this closure piece. You will now have two pieces of duct tape with an exposed closure strip in between.

4 Flip the taped closure piece over so the sticky sides of the strips of tape are facing up. Fold one of the pieces of tape over on itself lengthwise, leaving as much of the plastic closure strip as possible exposed. Seal with your fingers and repeat with the other piece of sticky tape.

> TIP!
>
> ## KEEP IT ZIPPED
>
> Don't let it slip your mind: If you flip the Ziploc closure pieces over the wrong way, they won't line up properly in the end, and the pouch won't close. To keep the sides of the Ziploc closure straight, mark the top of the Ziploc bag with a permanent marker before you begin.

5 To make the pouch, you will need to create a piece of easy duct tape fabric (see page 27) connected to each of the Ziploc closures. Stick a piece of tape ¼ inch wider than the width of the closure to the folded-over strips you made in step 4, overlapping by ¼ inch. Continue making your easy duct tape fabric hanging down from the closure until you reach the desired length.

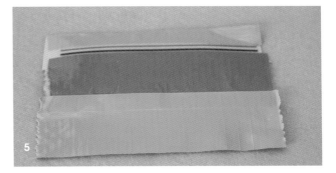

6 Repeat steps 2 through 5 with the second Ziploc closure piece. When you have 2 pieces of easy duct tape fabric with a Ziploc closure at the top, trim both pieces to the desired width and length. Trim slightly within the edges of the closure to make sure you get a clean edge.

7 Slide the Ziploc closure pieces back together. You now have 2 pieces of Ziploc closure fabric.

8 Seal the edges of your Ziploc closure fabric together using 1-inch strips of tape on all the open sides, like you did for the basic pouch on page 35. Use a few strips of tape to seal the top edges where the Ziploc closure pieces come together. Trim any excess.

Zipper Closure

LEVEL: ● ● ○ ○ ○ ┊ TIME: 15 minutes

MATERIALS

Zipper with bias tape or fabric attached

Duct tape

Scissors

Zippers are a secure way to close a bag or a wallet. You'll make the fabric on either side of the zipper, just like a Zip-loc closure on page 44, then build your project from there. If you're using a brand-new zipper, each side of the zipper will have fabric, called "bias tape," running down it. This is where you'll attach the duct tape. If you decide to use a repurposed zipper, make sure you leave a similar amount of fabric.

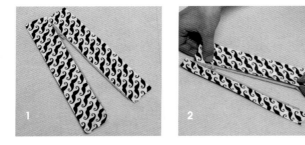

1 Open the zipper as far as it will go and place a strip of tape slightly longer than the bias tape over each side of the zipper, as close as you can get to the zipper itself without covering the teeth.

2 Flip the zipper over and fold the tape over on itself to seal in the bias tape. Do this on both sides of the zipper.

3 Now you can use the zipper closure on any project. When you add the closure to a pouch or purse, you'll need to seal each end of the zipper with some strips of duct tape to remove any gaps on the ends.

Velcro Closure

LEVEL: ● ○ ○ ○ ○ ⋮ **TIME: 5 minutes**

MATERIALS

Any duct tape project with a flap, such as a pouch

Sticky-backed Velcro

Scissors

Velcro is extremely effective as a closure, and just a tiny bit of it is all you need to keep a flap in place. Using sticky-backed Velcro ensures that you won't have to tape each Velcro piece in place.

1 Open the flap of the pouch and place a small square of the sticky-backed Velcro on the inside of the flap, centered and slightly in from the top edge, sticky side down.

2 Place a second, same-sized piece of Velcro on top of the first secured piece, sticky side up, so it grabs the first piece.

3 Close the flap and rub the edges with your fingers to help the sticky side of the Velcro adhere to the pouch. Open the flap and rub both sides of the Velcro to seal.

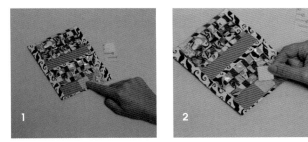

TIP!

BOTH SIDES NOW

Make sure you have both sides of the Velcro before you tape them down. You should have both a fuzzy side and a side with hooks.

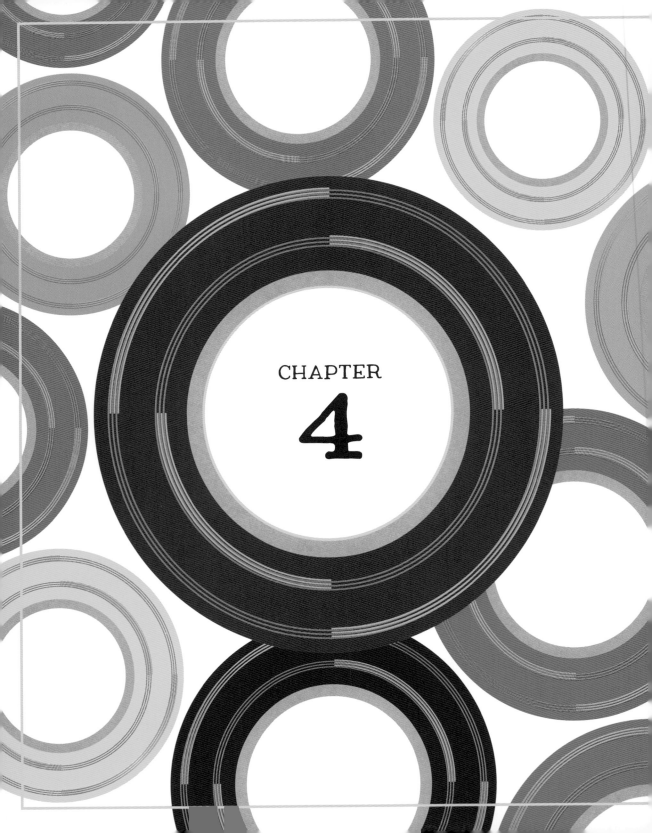

CHAPTER

4

QUICK
CRAFTS

Got a birthday party to go to but no gift wrap for the present? Quick! Make a Gift Bow (page 55)! Stuck inside on a rainy afternoon? Make a bouquet of duct tape Carnations (page 66) or Rosettes (page 60) and surprise someone you love. The quick crafts in Chapter 4 are the perfect projects for your crafting downtimes, plus they make fantastic embellishments for other projects. So grab some tape and get to it!

Tassel

LEVEL: ●●○○○ ¦ TIME: 10 minutes

MATERIALS
- -
Scissors

Duct tape

Tassels are great for embellishing everything from shoes to handbags to jewelry. Use them as key chains, luggage tags, and light pulls—almost anywhere you can imagine. Plus, you don't need a lot of duct tape to make a tassel, so they're great for extra bits of tape you have at the end of a project.

1 Make a 2-inch sticky strip (see page 26). If you want the tassel to be fuller, make the pieces longer. If you want it to be slim, cut shorter pieces. Leave about $1/4$ inch of the sticky side exposed on the long sides of the tape, as shown.

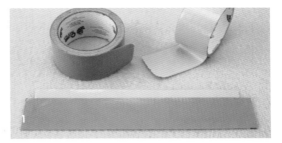

2 Fold one of the long overhanging sticky sides over to secure the 2 strips together. You will still have an exposed sticky bit of tape on the opposite long side. Trim any overhanging sticky bits of tape on the short ends of the strip so that the only sticky part showing is on the long side.

3 Very carefully make lots of little cuts in the long side of the tape almost up to the exposed sticky strip but not cutting all the way to the top. Continue cutting until the entire piece of tape looks like a piece of fringe.

4 Roll the fringed strip so that you're rolling the sticky exposed tape onto itself. This will help hold the tassel together. When you're done rolling, give the top of the tassel a good pinch to make sure the sticky tape is holding it together.

5 Wrap more tape around the top of the tassel to secure it. If you want to hang the tassel, use a thin fold-over strip (see page 24) to create a loop at the top.

Bow

LEVEL: ●●○○○ ⋮ TIME: 10 minutes

MATERIALS

Ruler
Duct tape
Scissors

There are tons of uses for a duct tape bow. Attach it to a pin and embellish your favorite jacket, tape it to your purse or clutch for some extra flair, or attach it to a Choker (page 170) to make a bow tie. Experiment with different colors and sizes of bows to really play up this fun embellishment.

1 To make a 3-inch-long bow, cut 2 strips of duct tape, one 6 inches long and one 7 inches long.

2 Lay the longer piece of tape sticky side up on the work surface. Place the shorter piece of tape on top of it, sticky sides together, leaving 1 inch of sticky tape showing on the short end of the longer piece.

3 Fold the short, sealed edge of the tape up to meet the opposite edge of the double thickness. Fold the sticky 1-inch flap of tape down onto it to secure the tape into a loop.

4 Now, cut a strip of duct tape 1/2 inch to 3/4 inches long for the center of the bow. This can be of a contrasting color or pattern, if you like.

5 Find the center of the loop and pinch the top and bottom edges together to form the bow shape. It might help to flatten the loop, fold it in half lengthwise, then fold each of the sides in half again in the shape of the letter *W*. This will help fan out either side of the loop so that it looks more bowlike.

6 Secure the middle of the bow with the strip of tape from step 4. You may want to add a second strip of tape to really hold the bow in place. There you go: a bow!

TIP!

A BOW FOR EVERY OCCASION

If you want to make a bow in a different size, just cut a piece of tape that is double the length of the desired finished bow size. The second piece of tape should be 1 inch longer than the first.

Gift Bow

LEVEL: ●●●○○ ┊ TIME: 30 minutes

MATERIALS

- - - - - - - - - - - - - - - - - - - -

Four 9-inch
Fold-Over Strips
(page 24)

Four 7-inch
Fold-Over Strips

2 1/2-inch
Fold-Over Strip

Hole punch

1 wire brad (at
least 1 inch long)

Add a decorative touch to your next gift with a duct tape gift bow. Not only are bows great for adorning packages, they also look adorable on purses, make handy luggage tags, and can even be used as a boutonniere for the duct tape prom.

1 Take one 9-inch fold-over strip and fold it into a loop, overlapping the two ends by 1 inch.

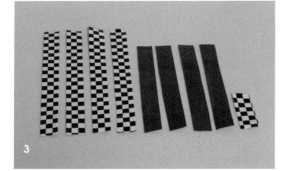

2 Pinch the entire loop together at the point where the ends overlap. Punch a hole through all 3 layers of tape exactly in the center of the 1-inch overlap. Lay flat again and set aside.

3 Repeat steps 1 and 2 with all of the 9-inch and 7-inch fold-over strips.

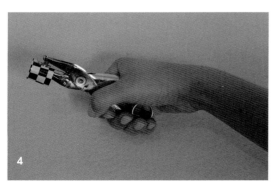

4 Now, wrap the 2 1/2-inch fold-over strip in a loop and punch a hole through the center of the overlap, but only through those 2 layers, not the third (top) layer like you did in step 2.

5 With the overlap still lined up, slip the legs of the brad through the holes in the 2 1/2-inch strip, with the button of the brad inside the loop and the legs on the outside.

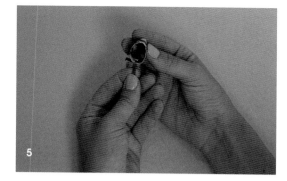

6 Starting with the 7-inch fold-over strips, begin layering the strips on top of each other on the legs of the brad: One at a time, slide the brad wires through the hole in the center of a strip, then fold each end in and thread onto the brad, overlapping to form the loop. Now, add the 9-inch strips using the same technique.

7 After sliding the last 9-inch strip onto the wires of the brad, open them up and push them tight against the last strip. Fluff up the strips and distribute them evenly to form a pretty bow.

VARY THE LENGTHS

To make a wild-and-crazy bow, make each fold-over strip a different length and vary the number of strips.

Fan-Fold Bow

LEVEL: ● ● ○ ○ ○ | TIME: 10 minutes

MATERIALS

7-by-6-inch piece of
Standard Duct Tape
Fabric (page 28)

Ruler

Scissors

This fan-fold bow is an alternative to the basic Bow (page 52). The fan-fold method creates a bow that tends to look fuller than the simpler traditional bow, so it's great for use in whimsical, colorful projects. Add a fan-fold bow as an embellishment on your favorite project, or simply attach one to a clip to make a fun hair accessory.

1 Make a piece of standard duct tape fabric
about 7 inches long by 6 inches wide. You can
alternate colors or patterns if you like.

2 Trim away any sticky pieces of tape that
extend beyond the rectangle of duct tape
fabric so that all sides of the fabric are even.
Next, tear a thin strip of duct tape a few inches
in length and set it aside. You'll use this piece
later to secure the center of the bow.

3 Begin folding the fabric accordion style.
Working back and forth, make equal-sized
narrow folds until the entire piece of fabric is
folded. You can experiment with larger folds or
very small folds to create different effects.

4 Pinch the fanned fabric in the center to create the bow shape. Now, take the thin strip
of duct tape from step 2 and wrap it around the
center of the bow to secure it.

Rosette

LEVEL: ● ● ● ● ○ ⋮ TIME: 20 minutes

MATERIALS

16-by-2-inch
Sticky Strip (best
to use two colors
of tape; page 26)

Duct tape

Scissors

Two 2-inch pieces
of Standard Duct
Tape Fabric
(page 28)

1 wire brad

X-acto knife

Dry-erase marker

Rosettes are a colorful, fun way to add the look of a flower to one of your projects. You can mix and match patterns, and even layer multiple rosettes to create amazing looks.

1 Fan-fold the sticky strip in $1/2$-inch folds with the sticky edge facing down (see step 3 on page 59).

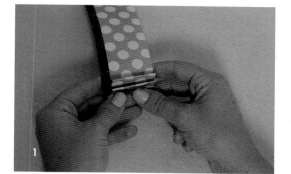

2 Open up the ends of the fan in a circle until they meet.

3 Using a small strip of tape in a matching color, tape the two ends of the strip together.

(see step 3 on page 59).

TIP!

VARY THE WIDTHS
Vary the size of the rosettes by varying the widths of the sticky strips.

4 Flip the rosette over and push the taped seam you just made slightly upward to flatten it out. Tape the folded-over edge in place with tape in a matching color and trim any excess tape.

5 Place a small square of tape in a matching color in the center of the back of the rosette. Using the scissors, cut tiny slits in the edges of the square of tape between each valley fold.

6 Smooth the flaps of tape down into the valleys. Repeat steps 5 and 6 on the other side of the rosette.

7 Now, cut the 2-inch pieces of duct tape into 1 1/2-inch circles.

8 Using the X-acto knife, make a small hole in the center of each circle and in the center of the rosette (use extreme caution).

9 Place the circle pieces on either side of the rosette and slide the wire brad through all three pieces, opening the brad arms across the back of the rosette to secure it in place.

10 Place a small piece of tape over the arms of the brad to keep them from scratching or catching on anything.

Layered Flower

LEVEL: ●○○○○ ⦙ **TIME:** 15 minutes

MATERIALS

Standard Duct Tape
Fabric (page 28)

Dry-erase marker

Scissors

X-acto knife

1 wire brad

L ayered flowers are a beautiful way to use up those last little bits of the duct tape roll. Try layering different shapes, such as triangles, squares, and rectangles, to create interesting geometric flowers. Attach your flower to a bag, tie, or wallet for an extra pop of color and style.

1 Trace the desired patterns and shapes onto the duct tape fabric with a dry-erase marker. Cut out the shapes.

2 Layer the shapes on top of each other to form a design.

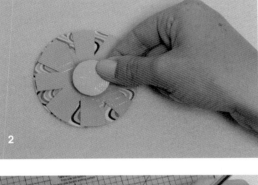

3 Use the X-acto knife to place a small cut in the center of the layers (use extreme caution).

4 Slip the legs of the wire brad down through the layers of tape to connect them. Once the brad is through all the layers, open the brad's arms to secure it in place.

Carnation

LEVEL: ● ● ● ● ○ ┊ TIME: 15 minutes

MATERIALS

6-by-16-inch piece of Standard Duct Tape Fabric (page 28)

16-inch piece of duct tape, plus more for finishing

Scissors

2 Leaves (page 73)

Pencil (optional)

Like the Rosettes (page 60), duct tape carnations look fantastic when they're gathered together in a bouquet. They also make nice pen toppers and are beautiful embellishments for hats.

1 Make the 6-by-16-inch piece of standard duct tape fabric into a large sticky strip (see page 26) by placing a 16-inch piece of duct tape along one edge, leaving 1 inch of sticky tape exposed.

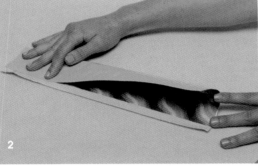

2 Fold the top edge of the sticky strip down so that it slightly overlaps the opposite sticky strip by about $1/2$ inch, leaving the other $1/2$ inch of sticky tape exposed. Run your finger along the edge to seal.

3 Cut very thin (about $1/8$ inch wide) 2-inch-long snips in the looped-over edge of the tape, like you would when making a tassel (see page 50). Be careful not to cut all the way through the sealed top edge of the strip.

4 Once the entire strip is cut, gently peel the sealed edge away from the sticky edge and fluff and spread apart the fringe you cut.

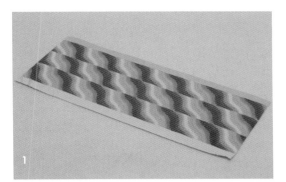

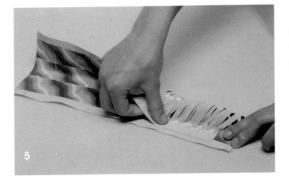

5 Once the fringe has been spread apart a bit, stick the bottom edge of the strip up onto the sticky edge again, like you did in step 2.

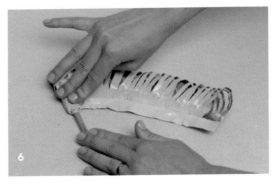

6 Roll the fringed strip so that you're rolling the sticky exposed tape onto itself, like you did with the tassel on page 50. If you're attaching the carnation to a pencil, simply place the end of the pencil on the sticky tape before you start rolling.

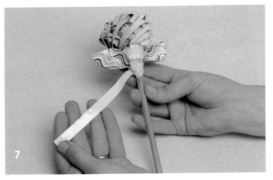

7 Add the leaves if you like, by following the instructions on page 73. And if you're attaching the carnation to a pencil, wrap the pencil with thin strips of stem-colored tape.

TIP!

BUDDING FLOWER
If you want a tighter, more clustered look for the carnation, skip steps 4 and 5.

8 Add a bit of grass by making a 5-by-1-inch sticky strip and cutting it like you would a tassel (page 50).

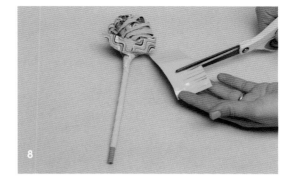

9 Wrap the grass around the base of the flower. Use extra tape to hold it in place, if necessary.

STICKY HIGH-FIVE

Jazmin, age 10, Pennsylvania
Jazmin came up with the idea of attaching a rose to the end of a pen to add some flair to an otherwise everyday writing instrument.

Rose Petal Flower

LEVEL: ● ● ● ○ ○ | TIME: 20 minutes

MATERIALS

Two 14-by-2-inch Sticky Strips (page 26)

Scissors

Parchment paper

Ruler

Dry-erase marker

2 Leaves (page 73)

Duct tape

Pencil (optional)

Rounded rose petals make this duct tape rose appear a bit more realistic than a Spike Rose (page 158). As you become more familiar with this project, you can begin to experiment with the number and size of the petals you use. Use fewer, smaller petals to make a simple flower, and use more, larger petals to make a beautifully blooming rose.

1 Lay the sticky strips lengthwise on the work surface, sticky side up, about ¹/2 inch apart. Cut a narrow strip of parchment paper and lay it lengthwise along the 2 sticky edges, connecting the strips, as shown. Press gently to seal.

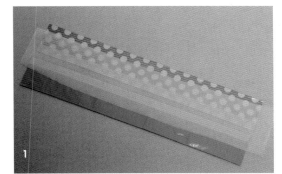

2 Cut both strips into 2-inch pieces. Cutting through the parchment paper will help keep the pieces the same size. You should end up with 14 square sticky strips.

3 Use the dry-erase marker to trace rounded petal shapes onto the squares and cut them out.

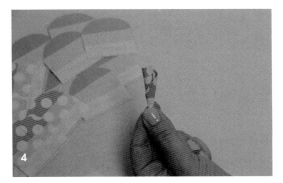

4 Remove the parchment paper from one of the petals and roll it on a slight diagonal angle, sticky side in, to make a cone, sealing the sticky end of the petal as you roll.

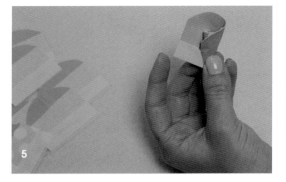

5 Now peel the parchment off the second petal. Attach one end of the sticky strip to the bottom of the cone, leaving a bit of the cone bottom showing. Pinch and wrap the second petal around the first cone. The pinching technique will give the flower a more realistic look.

6 Continue by placing additional petals on alternating sides, filling in any gaps as you go.

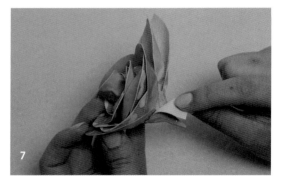

7 Once the rosebud is complete, attach the leaves to the base with thin strips of tape.

TIP!

ATTACHING TO A PENCIL
If you're attaching the rose to the end of a pencil, simply roll the first petal straight around the pencil, instead of in a cone shape.

Leaf

LEVEL: ● ○ ○ ○ ○ ¦ Less than 5 minutes

MATERIALS

6-by-2-inch piece of Standard Duct Tape Fabric (page 28)

Dry-erase marker

Scissors

Duct tape

You've already learned how to make a few kinds of duct tape flowers. Now, why not make some leaves to add to the base of your flowers? These leaves are simple to make and great for using up those last bits of the duct tape roll.

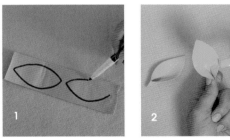

1 Draw leaf shapes on the standard duct tape fabric with the dry-erase marker and cut them out. You should be able to make 2 nice-size leaves per piece of fabric. Make a few smaller leaves, if you like.

2 Pinch one end of a leaf between your fingers and wrap the pinched end with a thin strip of duct tape to form the leaf shapes. Repeat with all the leaves.

3 To secure the leaf to the base of a flower or to another object, such as a pencil, attach a long, thin strip of duct tape to the bottom of the leaf, wrap the tape around the object, and attach it to the other side of the leaf to secure it.

Basic Sticker

LEVEL: ●○○○○ ┊ TIME: 5 minutes

MATERIALS

Simple artwork for tracing

Permanent marker

Parchment paper

Scissors

Duct Tape

Stickers can add another layer of detail or personalization to any project. Although store-bought stickers can be used in projects, duct tape stickers will adhere to projects much better and last much longer. Start out with this simple sticker, then move on to the Layered Sticker (page 76).

1 Using a permanent marker, trace the artwork onto a piece of parchment paper. Big, bold images work best.

2 Lay strips of duct tape over the design. Make sure to cover the design completely.

3 Flip the parchment paper over to see the design showing through the backside. Cut along the lines of the traced artwork to cut out the design.

4 Peel the parchment-paper backing away from the tape and place the sticker on whatever you wish to embellish.

STICKY HIGH-FIVE

Amanda K., age 9, California
Amanda submitted the idea for duct tape stickers after attending a duct tape-themed birthday party.

Layered Sticker

LEVEL: ●●○○○ ⦙ **TIME: 5 TO 30 MINUTES** (*or more*)

MATERIALS

Artwork for tracing

Permanent marker

Parchment paper

Scissors

Duct tape

Layered stickers can be as simple or complex as you like. Once you understand the technique of breaking objects down into their basic colors and shapes, you'll find that you can create amazing works of art with simple duct tape shapes. Layered stickers are also a great way to use any extra bits and snips you have left over from other projects.

1 Before you begin, divide the artwork into categories by color and number them.

2 Using a permanent marker, trace each element of the artwork onto the parchment paper. Group the elements of the artwork together by color.

3 Cover the parchment paper tracings with duct tape in their corresponding colors. Make sure you overlap the tape by ¹/4 inch, just as you would when making a piece of standard duct tape fabric (see page 28).

4 Flip the tape-covered parchment paper over and cut out the sticker pieces.

5 Peel the parchment paper backing away from each sticker and re-create the original artwork with the sticker pieces, starting with the bottom layer of the image first and working your way up to the top layer.

PROJECT
12

Ruffle

LEVEL: ●●●○○ ¦ TIME: 20 to 30 minutes

MATERIALS

18-by-2-inch Sticky Strip (page 26)

Ruler

Dry-erase marker

Duct tape

Scissors

This type of ruffle is best used for embellishing a flap or the edge of a purse or clutch. Ruffles require approximately three times as much tape as the length of the finished ruffle, so keep that in mind when you're budgeting the tape for projects.

1 Lay the sticky strip on the work surface, sticky side down. Make a ½-inch fan fold (see page 59) at one end of the strip. The finished ruffle will be one-third the length of the sticky strip, so for this project the 18-inch sticky strip will shorten to make a 6-inch ruffle.

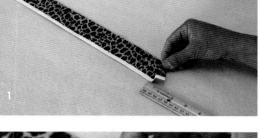

2 Leaving a ½-inch gap at the end of the first fold, create a second fan fold next to it. Continue folding in this way until you reach the end of the sticky strip. The sticky part of the strip will seal the pleats in place as you fold.

3 Take a 6-inch strip of tape and place it along the sticky edge of the ruffle, overlapping the ruffle by about ½ inch.

4 Secure the ruffle to the project with the 6-inch strip of tape. If you are placing your ruffle along the top edge of a bag, you can fold the extra tape over the edge for additional security.

STICKY HIGH-FIVE

Megan, age 12, Canada
Megan created a duct tape purse with both a ruffle and a braided strap, which provided inspiration for a number of projects.

CHAPTER

5

WALLETS

One of the first duct tape crafts to achieve widespread popularity was the duct tape wallet. The first wallets were often just basic pouches with a few slots to hold cards, but times (and designs) have changed since then. In Chapter 5, you'll find many different wallet designs that incorporate everything from ID holders to money and receipt pockets to intricate closure straps. Try making a few different kinds or combine your favorite techniques to design a wallet that's uniquely you.

PROJECT 13

Basic Wallet with Two Pockets

LEVEL: ● ● ○ ○ ○ ┊ TIME: 20 minutes

MATERIALS

9-by-9-inch piece of Standard Duct Tape Fabric (page 28)

Dry-erase marker

Scissors

Ruler

Duct tape

ID or credit card, for measuring

While a wallet can simply be an accessory that gets the job done, a duct tape wallet can be designed to fit your needs perfectly and express your personal style at the same time. Plus, making your own wallet out of duct tape will save you a trip to the department store and allow you to keep some of your hard-earned cash in that wallet. Follow these directions to create your own duct tape wallet, and see pages 86–98 for other versions of this standard money holder.

1 Measure 3 1/2 inches up from the bottom of the duct tape fabric and mark it with a dry-erase marker. Fold the bottom of the fabric up along this mark.

2 Fold the top of the fabric down so that its crease rests on the top of the bottom flap. The duct tape fabric should now resemble an envelope.

3 Cut a 4-inch-long piece of duct tape and cut or rip it in half lengthwise, creating two 4-inch strips of duct tape.

4 Seal the short edges of the envelope by laying the 4-inch strips over the open ends. The top flap of the envelope now forms a pocket on the front.

5 Flip the envelope over and fold the strips of tape onto themselves lengthwise to seal the ends.

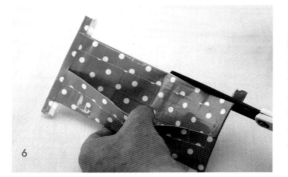

6 You now have a sealed envelope with a pocket on one side. Open the envelope back up by cutting all the way along the long top side. This will be the part of the wallet where you keep your money. Be sure that the top opening and the existing pocket both have their openings facing the same direction. Trim any overhanging corners of tape.

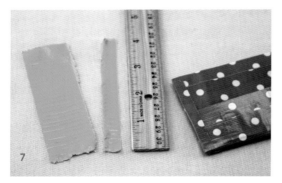

7 Now you'll create the individual wallet pockets for the cards. Begin by tearing off a strip of duct tape about 1/4 inch wide and a little longer than the width of the wallet.

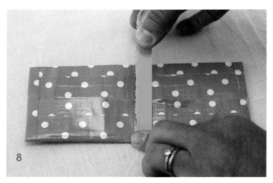

8 Fold the wallet in half and mark the center with a marker or by creasing it with your finger. Take the strip of duct tape and lay it down the center of the wallet, dividing the front pocket into 2 separate pockets. Tuck any overhanging tape inside the larger money pocket.

9 Snip the sealed tape edges where the pocket is formed to allow enough room for the cards. Depending on the size of the wallet, this may not be necessary. Test with the card to see if they will need more room.

Make a quick and easy wallet from a Basic Pouch (page 35).

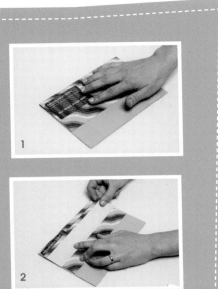

1. Place a credit card at the left edge of the pouch, approximately ¼ inch down from the top.

2. Place the sticky edge of a sticky strip under the bottom edge of the credit card and secure it in place on the pouch.

3. Add up to 2 more pockets this way, securing each sticky strip so the top edge is about ¼ inch under the one above it. Use the credit card to measure each pocket if you need to.

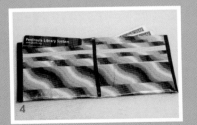

4. Fold the wallet in half and crease it along the middle. Open it back up and place a ¼-inch strip of tape along the crease to keep the cards from sliding into each other, tucking any tape inside the money holder.

PROJECT 14

Simple Clutch Wallet

LEVEL: ● ● ● ○ ○ ⋮ TIME: 30 to 45 minutes

MATERIALS

Four 4 1/2-inch
Fold-Over Strips
(page 24)

Scissors

Duct tape

6 1/2-by-13 1/2-inch
piece of Standard
Duct Tape Fabric
(page 28)

Ruler

Dry-erase marker

6 1/2-by-4 1/2-inch
piece of Standard
Duct Tape Fabric

The expanding accordion-fold sides make this clutch more than just a basic pouch. There's extra room in this clutch for your phone, your keys, or even a slim wallet. The accordion size can be adjusted simply by making the strip wider.

1 Fold each of the fold-over strips in half length-wise to make a valley fold (or long crease) in each.

2 Place a $1/2$-inch-wide strip of tape on either side of each valley fold , overlapping by about $1/4$ inch, to make two-sided sticky strips. The sticky side should be facing out.

3 On the $6\,1/2$-by-$13\,1/2$-inch piece of duct tape fabric, measure and mark $4\,1/2$ inches and 9 inches lengthwise. Fold and crease the fabric at these marks.

4 Stick the sticky edge of one of the fold-over strips to the underside of the fabric between the two marks you just made. The peak of the valley fold should be facing up. Repeat with another fold-over strip along the opposite edge of the fabric.

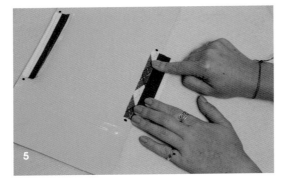

5 Take a very thin strip of tape and place it along the seam where the fabric and the valley fold meet. Trim any excess tape. Repeat with the other fold-over strip.

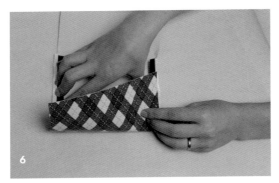

6 Fold the fold-over strip back on itself so the sticky side faces up and hangs over the edge of the fabric. Fold the lower flap of the fabric up and line its edge up with the fold-over strip. The sticky part of the strip should be exposed along the outside edge.

7 Fold the sticky tape over the edge of the fabric and secure on both sides.

8 You now have a clutch with a single accordion fold on each side. Use the 4 ½-x-6 ½-inch piece of duct tape fabric to create another pocket on the front of the pouch. Attach the two remaining fold-over strips to the outside edges of the clutch, then repeat steps 5 through 7 to attach the piece of additional fabric to the front of the pouch.

9   Seal the bottom of the clutch with a 1-inch strip of duct tape and trim any excess tape.

10   You can add as many accordion folds as you like in the same manner you did in step 8, or stop after two folds, as shown here.

STICKY HIGH-FIVE

Karly, age 11, Utah
Karly combined a wallet and a change purse to make an extra-special (and extra-useful) wallet.

Multipocket Wallet

LEVEL: ●●●○○ ┊ TIME: 30 to 45 minutes

MATERIALS

ID or credit card
for measuring

Three 2-by-4-inch
Sticky Strips
(page 26)

Two 2-by-4-inch
pieces of Stan-
dard Duct Tape
Fabric (page 28)

Duct tape

Scissors

3 1/2-by-2 1/2-inch
Clear Window
(page 34)

7-by-9-inch piece
of Standard Duct
Tape Fabric

3 1/2-by-9-inch
piece of Standard
Duct Tape Fabric

This version of a standard wallet has hidden pockets for additional cards under the
ID holder and the credit card holder. The
pouch is also divided in half, creating pockets
for both money and receipts.

Make the Credit Card Holder

1 Place the ID or credit card along the edge of one of the sticky strips where the fabric side meets the sticky side.

2 Turn the sticky strip with the card sticky side down on one of the 2-by-4-inch pieces of duct tape fabric so that the credit card lines up with the top edge of the fold-over strip. Secure the sticky strip.

3 Line up the other 2 sticky strips below the first one, each ¹/₄ inch below the one above it.

4 Secure the left-hand edges of the card-holder pockets with a full strip of tape, making sure you leave enough room for the cards to fit in your pockets.

5 Fold the securing tape over on the back and trim any excess tape.

Make the ID Holder Pocket

1 Place a ¹/2-inch strip of duct tape lengthwise across the top of the clear window. Wrap any extra length of tape around the backside of the window and trim it.

2 Place ¹/2-inch strips of duct tape along the two shorter sides of the window, with half of the tape on the window and half hanging over the sides.

3 Center the window on the second 2-by-4-inch piece of duct tape fabric and secure the two sticky sides to the fabric. Add a last strip of tape on the bottom to secure the window on three sides, leaving the top sealed edge open.

Thicker Strips

To make a sticky strip that is wider than 2 inches, add width by adding layers of tape using the same technique you used to create duct tape fabric (see pages 27 and 28).

Attach the Card Holders

1 Lay out two 1-by-10-inch strips of duct tape on the work surface. Place the ID window and the credit card holder along the top edge of the 7-by-9-inch piece of duct tape fabric. Line the ID window up with the left-hand corner and the credit card holder with the right-hand corner.

2 Secure the bottom edges of the holders to the fabric with one of the 1-by-10-inch strips. Repeat along the top edge, leaving a 1/2 inch of the sticky side of the tape hanging over. You may need to clip the card pockets as you did for the basic wallet (see page 84, step 9).

3 Flip the fabric over and fold the sticky pieces of tape over onto the back of the fabric. Trim any excess tape.

Finish the Wallet

1 Place the 3 1/2-by-9-inch piece of fabric at the top edge of the 7-by-9-inch piece of fabric and fold up the bottom end of the 7-by-9-inch piece of fabric to form a pouch, enclosing the 3 1/2-by-9-inch piece of fabric.

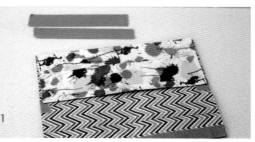

2 Seal the short edges of the wallet with strips of tape as you would a basic pouch (see page 35) and trim any overhanging pieces of tape.

Advanced Clutch Wallet

LEVEL: ●●●●○ | **TIME: 30 to 45 minutes**

MATERIALS

Five 7-by-4-inch pieces of Standard Duct Tape Fabric (page 28)

Duct tape

Scissors

Two to five 2-by-4-inch Sticky Strips (page 26)

ID or credit card for measuring

Clear Window (page 34)

Standard key for measuring

Dry-erase marker

Ruler

Double-Folded Strip (page 25)

A wallet can simply be a place to hold your money, but it can also be a carryall for your ID card, frequent-sandwich-buyer punch card, house key, and more. Use your favorite duct tape and follow these instructions to create your own personalized clutch wallet, complete with an ID pocket and a little pocket for your key.

1 Place one piece of the duct tape fabric directly on top of another, and use a tape in a contrasting color to seal them together along both of the shorter sides and one of the longer sides to make a pocket. Repeat with two other pieces of duct tape fabric to make 2 pockets from 4 pieces of the fabric.

2 Line up the sticky edge of one of the sticky strips with a short edge of one of the pouches to make the first card holder pocket. Use a card as a measuring device to add the next sticky strip underneath and above the bottom of that sticky strip. Leave about 1/2 inch of space between pockets so you can easily remove the cards. This is a good opportunity to alternate patterns or colors of tape if you like.

3 Continue to add as many card pockets as you like, as long as you're sure you don't crowd them, and making sure the final card doesn't stick out over the top of the pouch. Seal the sides of the pockets in place with a thin strip of tape. When sealing the opened edge of the wallet, tuck the tape inside the pocket so you don't seal the money holder closed.

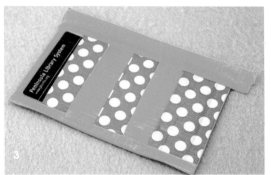

4 To make the ID pocket, fold a strip of duct tape over one of the long ends of the clear window to seal that edge. Secure the window of the pouch with 3 small strips of duct tape, leaving the side you just sealed open so you can slide your ID in and out, and positioning it on one half of the pouch to leave room for the key pocket.

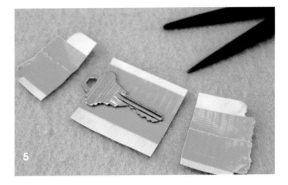

5 To make the key pocket, use a standard key as the template for sizing it. The top of the key can stick out of the pocket a little. Cut 2 pieces of duct tape, one sized to the key and one 1/2 inch shorter in width. Attach 2 pieces of tape on the sticky sides together, leaving 1/4 inch on either side and lining up the top and bottom.

6 Flip the key pocket over and secure it to the pouch next to the ID pocket. Add a thin strip of tape to seal the bottom of the key pocket. Seal the top edge of the pocket with another small trim of duct tape (a contrasting tape looks nice, as in the photo), folding the top strip over the top of the pocket like you did in step 4.

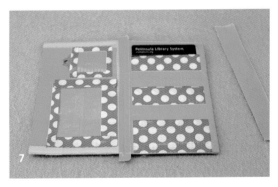

7 Now, it's time to put the 2 large pockets together to create the wallet. Make sure that both have their open (money) side facing out. Lay them side by side, long sides together, on the work surface, with about 1/4 inch of space between. Attach the 2 sides to each other with a thin piece of duct tape down the center. Do this on both the front and the back of the wallet.

8 Next, create a flap using the fifth piece of duct tape fabric you made in step 1. Fold the fabric in half and draw a design of your choice on it. Be sure to leave a tab at least 1 1/2 inches long for the closure. Cut out the design.

9 Attach the flap to the wallet the same way you connected the 2 halves of the wallet in step 7. After attaching both sides of the flap, close the wallet and determine where to place the closure.

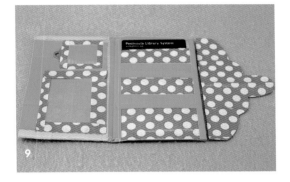

10 To create the flap closure, place the double-folded strip just over the tab you've created. Make sure there's enough room underneath so the tab will stay shut but can also be opened easily. Secure the closure to the wallet on both sides with 2 small pieces of tape. Now, you can decorate and embellish the wallet however you like!

TIP!

MIND THE GAP
When connecting pieces of duct tape fabric, it's best to keep the gap between them as small as possible: 1/4 inch works just fine, but 1/8 inch will make your project even stronger.

Trifold Wallet with ID Holder

LEVEL: ●●●○○ ¦ TIME: 30 to 45 minutes

MATERIALS

8-by-9-inch piece
of Standard Duct
Tape Fabric
(page 28)

Dry-erase marker

Ruler

ID or credit card
for measuring

Eight 2-by-4-inch
Sticky Strips
(page 26)

Scissors

Duct tape

3³/4-by-2¹/2-inch
Clear Window
(page 34)

This type of wallet can be designed to fit your specific needs. This version has eight credit card pockets, an ID holder, and a large pouch for cash, but you can add as many or as few card pockets as you like, remove the ID holder, or adapt the design in another way to fit your needs.

1 Fold the duct tape fabric in half along the 8-inch side to make a 9-by-4-inch wallet. Measure and mark the wallet at 3 and 6 inches lengthwise.

2 Lay a credit card slightly in front of one short edge of the wallet. Attach the sticky edge of a sticky strip along the bottom of the card. Make sure the sticky edges of your strips are only 1/4-inch wide so you can fit them on the wallet.

3 Add 3 more sticky strips, each one 1/4 inch in from the other, until you reach the 3-inch mark. Make sure the top of the credit card does not stick out past the 3-inch mark.

4 Repeat on the other end of the duct tape fabric, until you reach the 6-inch mark. The card pockets should open toward the center of the wallet.

5 Unfold the fabric and seal the outer edges of the card pockets using a $1/2$-inch strip of tape. Seal the opposite end of the fabric in the same way. Trim any excess tape.

6 Refold the wallet. Seal 1 of the shorter edges of the clear window with a piece of $1/2$-inch tape. Center the window between the 3-inch and 6-inch marks, with the sealed edge of the window directly under the newly sealed pocket edge. Attach the 2 longer sides of the window to the fabric with $1/2$-inch strips of tape.

7 Use another $1/2$-inch strip of tape to seal the bottom of the pockets and the ID window to the fabric.

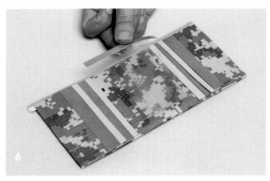

8 Seal the short edges of the wallet with $1/2$-inch strips of tape to finish the wallet. Trim any overhanging tape.

Checkbook Keeper

LEVEL: ●●●○○ ⦙ TIME: 15 to 20 minutes

MATERIALS

Checkbook for measuring

Standard Duct Tape Fabric in desired size (page 28)

9-inch Double-Folded Strip (page 25)

Pen

Checkbook inserts

Duct tape

Scissors

Dry-erase marker

Ruler

This checkbook holder uses a pen as a closure, so you'll never be without a pen for writing checks. The size of the fabric for this project depends on the size of your inserts (the actual checks and the register). Measure the inserts' width and length. Multiply the width by 4 and add ¼ inch to the length to determine the size of the fabric.

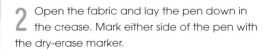

1 Fold the duct tape fabric in half widthwise and crease it.

2 Open the fabric and lay the pen down in the crease. Mark either side of the pen with the dry-erase marker.

3 Line up 1 long edge of each checkbook insert or template with the mark next to the pen. Mark where the bottom edge of each insert lies with a dry-erase marker.

4 Fold the bottom of the fabric up to the mark and secure the edges with $1/2$-inch pieces of tape, forming a pocket. Repeat with the top flap and trim any excess tape.

5 Cut the double fold-over strip into three 3-inch pieces.

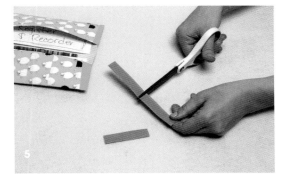

6 Fold the strips into pen-sized loops and attach them to the flaps of the fabric, 1 strip centered and secured on the bottom pocket and 2 strips on the top pocket, on either side of the center loop.

7 Slide the cardboard backing of the check inserts into the bottom pocket and the cardboard backing of the check register into the top pocket. Close the pouch and secure with the pen through the loops.

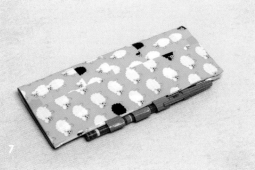

TIP!

STORING EXTRA TAPE

When your duct tape is going to be out of commission for a while, be sure to fold over the end. This makes it much easier to start the roll again quickly and without getting that silly, long half-piece tear.

CHAPTER

6

PURSES, BAGS, AND CASES

Duct tape is strong, durable, and malleable, which makes it the perfect material for making cases, purses, and clutches—anything you need to keep your stuff safe. It's also colorful, which means that anything you make out of duct tape will look unique and personalized—no two projects are ever the same! In Chapter 6, you'll learn to make all kinds of cases, from decorative purses to heavy-duty electronics holders. Once you get the basic techniques down, personalize them even more with embellishments, such as bows, stickers, and anything else you like.

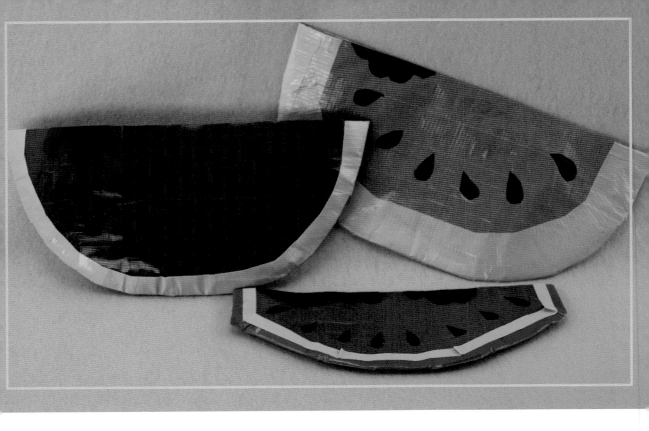

Watermelon Purse

LEVEL: ● ● ● ● ○ ┊ TIME: 30 to 45 minutes

MATERIALS

Two 14-by-8-inch pieces of Standard Duct Tape Fabric, one green and one red (page 28)

Templates in the shape of a large half circle, seeds, and bite marks (page 236)

Duct tape in green and black

Scissors

Parchment paper

Permanent marker

2 small magnets, or Velcro, for closure (optional)

Ribbon for handle (optional)

Fold-Over Strip (page 24)

Why carry an ordinary purse when you can carry a juicy, fun watermelon purse? Use your favorite shades of red, pink, and green duct tape for this project. You can also use the basic steps you learn from this project to create your own purse in a different shape. The possibilities are endless!

1 Trace the half-circle template onto both the green and red sheets of duct tape fabric.

2 Cut out the half circles. The red fabric will be the front of the purse, and the green will be the back. Lay the red piece on top of the green piece.

3 Now, cut about a dozen 1- to 2-inch strips of green duct tape and set them aside. You'll use these in the next few steps.

4 Place 1 green strip of tape in the middle of the curved edge of the watermelon slice, with half of the strip hanging over the edge.

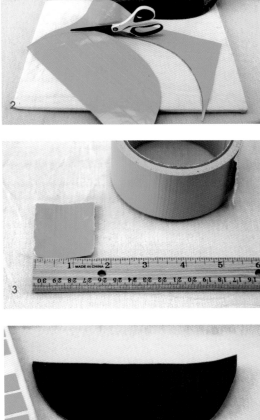

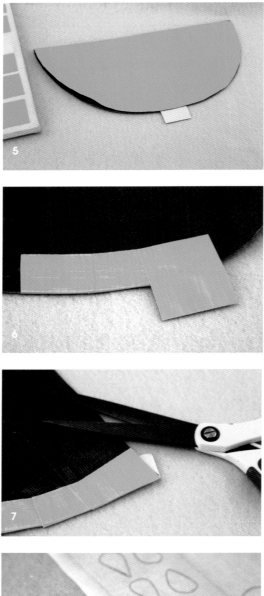

5 Flip the purse over and fold the hanging strip over onto the green side, attaching the two pieces.

6 Flip the purse back over so the red side is facing up. Take another strip of green tape and place it on the red side so that it just overlaps with the first strip. Keep the top edges of the strips even, because this green border will be the watermelon purse's "rind." Flip the purse over to the green side, and fold the strip over in the same way you folded the first one.

7 Continue laying strips along the curved edge of the purse until you reach the straight edge at the top. Once you reach the top, use the scissors to trim away any excess tape.

8 Next, you'll create the watermelon seeds and bite mark. Trace around the seeds and bite-mark templates on a piece of parchment paper. Cover the paper with black duct tape, and when you flip it over, you'll be able to see the shapes through the paper. Cut out the shapes.

9 Peel the parchment paper off the seeds and bite-mark stickers and arrange the stickers on the red side of the purse.

10 To cover up any exposed stickiness on the inside seam of the purse, cut a few small strips of duct tape and line the inside seam with them.

11 You now have a watermelon-style pouch. You can leave the purse like this or attach a closure to make it a clutch (see pages 38–47 for closures). You can also add straps to the purse either by duct-taping a length of ribbon to the inside of the pouch or by attaching a long fold-over strip (see page 24).

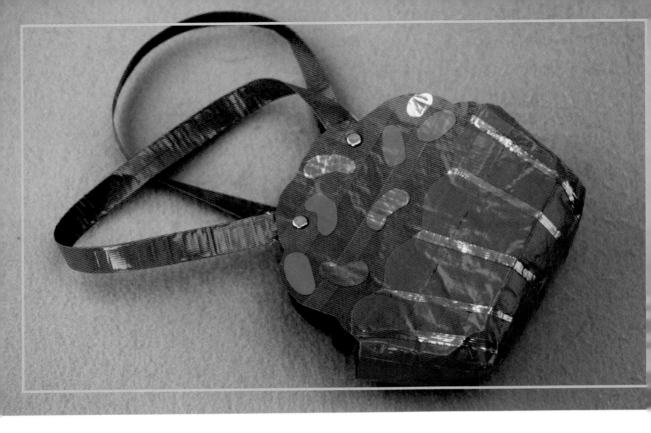

Cupcake Purse

LEVEL: ●●●●○ | TIME: 30 to 45 minutes

MATERIALS

Cupcake template (page 237)

Scissors

Tarp

Permanent marker

Duct tape

Hole punch

Brads

Parchment paper

2 small magnets, or Velcro, for closure (optional)

A cupcake purse is a sweet way to carry around your phone, keys, and wallet. You can decorate your cupcake for every occasion, from a fancy dinner to an afternoon in the park. Match your frosting to your favorite outfit and you're ready to go!

1 Trace or photocopy the cupcake template onto 2 sheets of paper. Cut out the 2 templates and tape them together on their long straight sides.

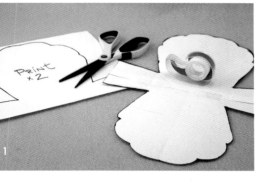

2 Cut out a rectangle of tarp slightly larger than the pattern and trace the pattern onto the tarp.

3 Choose the 2 duct tape colors you'll use for the base and frosting of the cupcake. Cover the tarp with strips of these tapes, starting from the center. You don't need to cover the entire piece of tarp, only everything inside the lines of the pattern. Try to match both sides of the cupcake exactly, like a mirror image.

4 Once the pattern is completely covered with tape, lay the template back down on top of the tape and trace it again so you can see the lines. Cut out the purse piece.

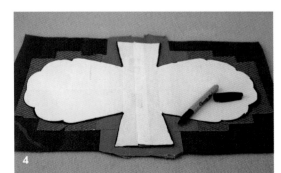

5 Fold the sides of the purse piece up to create the shape of the cupcake base, and connect the base corners together with tape in the same color you used to create the base. Secure all 4 sides and trim any excess tape.

6 Reinforce the inside corners of the purse with strips of duct tape.

7 Make two double-folded strips between 12 to 16 inches long. These will be the straps of the purse.

8 Round off the edges of the straps and punch a hole in each end. Punch holes in the top corners of the purse where you want to attach the straps.

9 Thread the wires of the brads through the holes in the straps and the purse from the outside in. Open the wires flat to attach the straps. If you're using long brads, you may want to fold the brad wires back on themselves.

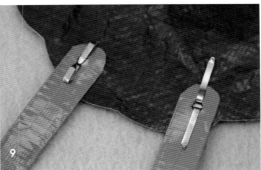

10 Now it's time to start decorating! Draw any designs you want to go on the cupcake—like sprinkles, a candle, or anything else—on the parchment paper. Use duct tape to make stickers (see page 74) and place them on the purse anywhere you like.

11 Decorate the base of the cupcake by cutting strips of tape to create the ridges of a cupcake liner.

12 You can either leave the top of the purse open or close it with a closure. See pages 38–47 for closure directions. Now you have a sweet purse!

PROJECT
21

Makeup Case

LEVEL: ● ● ● ○ ○ | TIME: 15 minutes

MATERIALS

Zipper Closure
(page 46)

Duct tape

Scissors

Stickers (page 74),
jewels, markers, etc,
for embellishing

Duct tape is the perfect material to use for a makeup case because it's durable, it's stain resistant, and it will keep any accidental makeup spills from leaking into other parts of your bag. If you don't have a zipper, a Ziploc closure (page 44) is a good alternative way to keep your stuff secure.

1 Attach strips of tape to one side of the zipper closure to make duct tape fabric for the pouch.

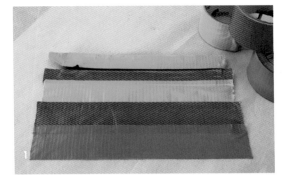

2 Flip the zipper and duct tape over and cover the sticky side of the tape with more strips, sticky side down, to complete the duct tape fabric piece. Repeat on the other side of the zipper closure so that you have 2 pieces of duct tape fabric attached to the zipper. Trim the edges of the pieces of fabric.

3 Now, seal the edges of the bag. Seal the sides first and then the bottom so that the sides line up correctly. Make sure to seal the open edges of the zipper without covering the ends so the zipper can still open and close. Seal any inside sticky edges with thin strips of tape.

4 Finish the bag with embellishments of duct tape stickers, stripes made of duct tape, jewels, etc.

Sunglasses Case

LEVEL: ●●●○○ | **TIME:** 15 minutes

MATERIALS

Sunglasses for measuring

Piece of felt about three times as long as your sunglasses

Permanent marker

Ruler

Scissors

Duct tape

Sticky-backed Velcro

This sunglasses case is made from felt-backed duct tape fabric to keep your sunglasses from getting scratched or broken. Sunglasses have a tendency to get lost, so make your case out of bright, colorful duct tape so it's easier to find if you do lose it.

1 Place the sunglasses down on the piece of felt and mark a rectangle around them that is three times longer and 1 inch wider than the sunglasses. Cut out the rectangle.

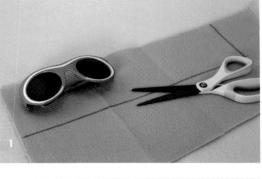

2 Cover one side of the felt with duct tape. The tape should overhang each side of the felt by about 1 inch. Fold the overhanging tape on the short ends back onto the felt.

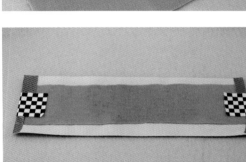

3 Measure the length of the sunglasses plus 1/2 inch from one of the ends of the felt and mark it. Cover the opposite end with a 2-inch strip of duct tape to make the flap.

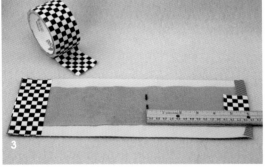

4 Fold the case in half at the point you just marked. The top edge should meet the bottom edge of the flap. If not, add another strip of tape so that the two edges meet. The sticky pieces of tape along the sides will stick together, forming a pouch. Trim away the excess tape, being careful not to cut into the felt. Trim the flap into the desired shape.

5 Reinforce the side seams of the case with 1-inch strips of duct tape.

6 Attach a small square of the sticky-backed Velcro to the closure flap and press it onto the case to secure it in place.

HOOK IT ON
To hook your sunglasses onto your belt, follow steps 3-4 for the Money Keeper (page 122).

Checkerboard Beach Bag

LEVEL: ● ● ● ● ◐ | TIME: 2 hours

Once you've mastered the weaving technique (see page 32),
this project is just a matter of assembling a few pieces. This checkerboard bag is roomy and strong—perfect for carrying books, groceries, or beach supplies. Make the bag any size you like by adjusting the size of the woven duct tape fabric.

MATERIALS

Two 10-by-10-inch pieces of Woven Duct Tape Fabric (page 32)

Three 5-by-10-inch pieces of Woven Duct Tape Fabric

Two 4-foot-long Super-Strong Strips (page 25)

Duct tape

Hole punch (optional)

Brads (optional)

1 Lay out the pieces of woven duct tape fabric in the following pattern from left to right: 10-inch piece, 5-inch piece, 10-inch piece, 5-inch piece. Place one 5-inch piece lengthwise along the bottom of the second 10-inch piece. You should leave about ¹/4 inch of space between each piece of duct tape fabric.

2 Connect all the pieces of fabric together with 1-inch strips of duct tape.

3 Flip the connected pieces of fabric over and repeat step 2 so that all the seams are sealed. Trim any excess tape.

4 Flip the fabric back over and fold the 4 pieces of fabric that are taped in a long line into a box, for the shape of the bag. The remaining hanging piece of fabric is the bottom of the bag. Tape the remaining unsealed long side of the box on both the inside and the outside of the bag.

5 Now, fold the bottom of the bag into place and tape the sides to seal them. Tape the seams on the inside of the bag, too. Place 1-inch tape pieces around the bottom of the bag for extra security.

6 Next, attach straps to the bag. To make the straps extra strong, overlap two 9-inch strips of tape lengthwise on top of the end of the strap, and place a third strip of tape over the overlap. Do this for each end of each strap, and tape them to the inside of the bag at each corner.

7 Alternatively, you can attach the straps with brads. Simply punch holes in the four corners of the bag and in the end of each strap, and connect them with brads.

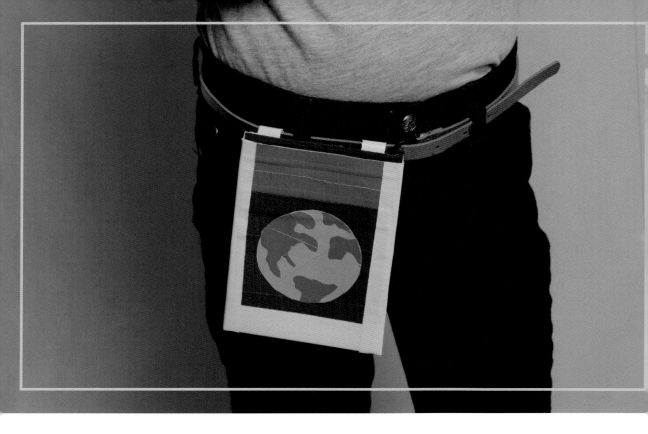

Money Keeper

LEVEL: ● ● ● ○ ○ ┊ TIME: 45 minutes

MATERIALS

Ziploc bag

Two 4½-by-6 inch pieces of Ziploc Closure fabric (page 44)

3 ½-by-5-inch piece of Standard Duct Tape Fabric (page 28)

Scissors

Duct tape

Two 8-inch Double-Folded Strips (page 25)

Permanent marker

This little bag has a hidden inside pocket and two Ziploc closures to keep your money and important documents (like a passport) safe. This version is designed to attach to a belt, but your money keeper can also be worn on a string or elastic around your neck and tucked away under your shirt. A money keeper is perfect for traveling, but it's also handy for everyday use if you don't want to carry a purse or a wallet.

1 The two pieces of Ziplock closure fabric will form the outside of the money keeper pouch. To make the inner hidden pocket, place one piece of Ziploc closure fabric, ridged side up, on the work surface. Center the 3½-by-5-inch piece of duct tape fabric on top of the piece of Ziploc closure fabric, below the closure, making sure there is a border of at least ½ inch of closure fabric on the other 3 sides. Trim the duct tape fabric if necessary.

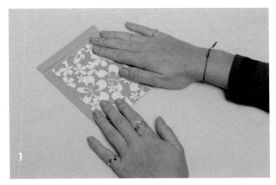

2 Connect the 3 open sides of the Ziploc closure fabric and the duct tape fabric using 1-inch strips of tape. Leave the top edge under the Ziploc closure unsealed.

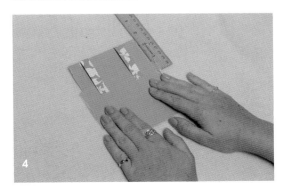

3 Next you'll add the straps to the money keeper to attach it to your belt. Flip the fabric with the hidden pocket over. Lay the 2 double-folded strips on the back of the hidden pocket fabric, about 1 inch in from the sides. Half of the strips should be on the fabric, and half should be sticking out above it. Secure both of the straps in place with duct tape.

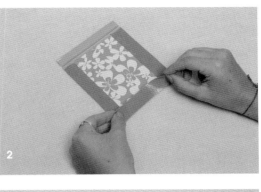

4 Fold the straps down on the same side of the fabric to form loops. Secure the ends of the straps with tape, leaving about 2½ inches of strap loose so the belt can slip through. The back of the pouch is now finished. Set this piece aside.

5 Place the remaining piece of Ziploc closure fabric on the work surface with the ridged side of the closure facing down. Remove the closure from the Ziploc bag (see step 1 on page 44) and trim the closure to the width of the fabric. Slip the closure apart, marking with arrows (see step 2 on page 44), and set one of the closure pieces aside.

6 Center one of the closure pieces on the fabric, ridged side up and with the arrow pointing toward the top of the fabric. Secure the top and bottom of the closure piece with 1-inch strips of duct tape.

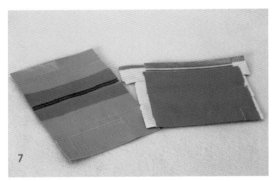

7 Take the other closure piece and make a piece of Ziploc closure fabric (see page 44) that will attach to the strip you just taped down and complete the front part of the pouch. Slide the closures together to connect the two pieces of fabric.

8 Trim any excess tape from the fabric you just made so it matches the size of the Ziploc closure fabric.

9 Now, it's time to put all the pieces of the money keeper together. Slide the two large pieces of Ziploc closure fabric together, with the straps on the outside, the hidden pocket sandwiched between the fabric, and the second Ziploc-sealed pocket on the front.

10 Secure the two sides and the bottom of the pouch with 1-inch strips of duct tape like you did in step 1. This will seal both the front pocket in place and the sides of the entire pouch at the same time. Slide the belt through the loops on the back of the money keeper and attach it around your waist.

TIP!

MORE BANG FOR YOUR DUCT

There are tons of ways to stretch your duct tape dollars. You can make the same amount of fabric with half the amount of tape by using a backing material like tarp or felt (see pages 30 and 31). Also, save every last bit of the roll! Keep any stray bits and snips to use as stickers, embellishments, or to create a collaged piece of duct tape fabric.

Smartphone Case

LEVEL: ●●●○○ | **TIME:** 20 minutes

MATERIALS

Smartphone for measuring

3-by-16-inch piece of Felt-backed Duct Tape Fabric (page 31)

Ruler

Scissors

Permanent marker

Wire hanger

Wire cutters

Needle-nose pliers

Duct tape

Hole punch

Smartphones are great for texting, calling, and surfing the Web, but once you get a crack in that screen, they're not quite so useful anymore, and they're expensive to fix or replace. Protect your precious phone with this smartphone case made out of felt-backed duct tape fabric. This case also features a handy wire hook so you can attach your phone to your belt or bag.

1 Place the phone on the felt-backed duct tape fabric flush with the bottom edge. Flip the phone over along the tape lengthwise to measure 2 phone lengths on the duct tape fabric. This will be the basis of the pouch. Flip the phone one more time to see how long you should make the flap. Mark the fabric at the end of 3 phone lengths and trim any excess tape.

2 Place the phone in the center of the fabric. Fold up the bottom of the fabric to form the pouch. If you leave a little bit of the phone sticking out of the top of the pouch, it will be easier to grab. Mark the top of the fold on the duct tape fabric.

3 From that marked point, measure 1 inch down and make a mark on the fabric at that point long enough to cross the center.

4 Fold the fabric in half lengthwise and cut a small snip at the center mark you made to create a hole in the center of the fabric.

5 Now, take the wire hanger and squeeze the sides together to form a tight U-shaped bend. With the wire cutters, snip off the U-shaped piece so that it is about 3 to 4 inches long.

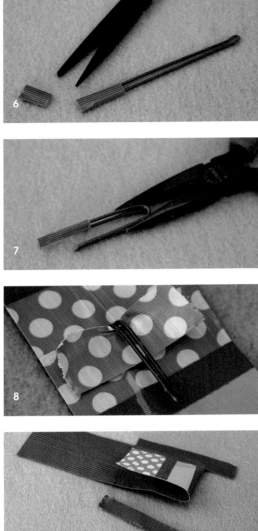

6 With the needle-nose pliers, squeeze the U-bend together even tighter. Cover the sharp ends with duct tape, wrapping it around and around to seal the ends in. This eliminates any sharp edges that could scratch the phone.

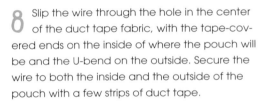

7 With the needle-nose pliers, bend the wire in half again so that the U-bend curves up toward the duct tape–covered ends.

8 Slip the wire through the hole in the center of the duct tape fabric, with the tape-covered ends on the inside of where the pouch will be and the U-bend on the outside. Secure the wire to both the inside and the outside of the pouch with a few strips of duct tape.

9 Fold the duct tape fabric up to form the pouch again, bringing the bottom of the fabric to the mark you made earlier. Seal the sides lengthwise with small strips of duct tape. Trim off any excess tape.

STICKY HIGH-FIVE

Amanda H., age 23, Ohio
Amanda's creative ideas took the Smartphone Case and Tablet Case (page 130) to the next level.

10 Now you'll flatten the bottom of the pouch so the phone will fit neatly inside. Slip the phone into the pouch, then pinch the bottom corner of the pouch so that it forms a tri-angle. Fold the triangle over so that it lays flat on the bottom of the pouch. Secure it with a small piece of tape, and repeat with the other corner.

11 In order to keep the flap securely closed, you'll need to add a strap across the pouch that the flap can slide under. Make a double-folded strip (see page 25) as long as your pouch is wide. Place the strap across the front of the pouch, about a third of the way down from the top. Secure the sides with tape.

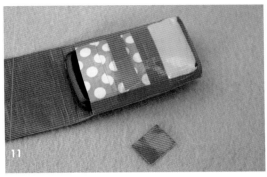

12 Trim the end of the flap into any shape that you want. Just make sure it still fits under the closure strap.

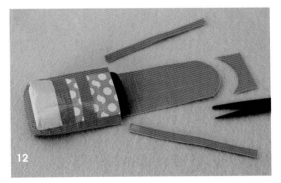

13 Now add a hole where the headphone jack connects to your device. To do this, slide the phone inside the case and close the flap. Press the flap down on the top of the phone until you feel where the headphone jack is; pressing down will leave an impression on the tape. On that impression, use the hole punch to make a hole in the flap.

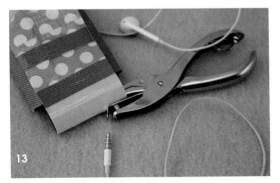

Tablet Case

LEVEL: ●●●●● | **TIME: 90 MINUTES**

MATERIALS

Tablet, for measuring

2 corrugated cardboard pieces cut to the size of your device

Duct tape

4 Super-Strong Strips a bit longer than the longest side of your device (page 25)

X-acto knife

Scissors

Dry-erase marker

4-by-2-inch Double-Folded Strip (page 25)

Sticky-backed Velcro

A tablet is a great device to have, but carrying it around can be nerve-wracking, since it is a delicate piece of machinery and can get scratched or cracked with one wrong move. Make this tablet case to protect your tablet at home and on the go. Each tablet design is different, so make sure you have your tablet handy when you're making this project to check the size and placement of the buttons.

1 Cover the cardboard pieces completely with duct tape, front and back. Make sure each of the edges is smooth and sealed.

2 To create the binding spine, place the two pieces of cardboard side by side with a $3/4$-inch gap between them. Connect the pieces of cardboard along their long sides with three 4-inch pieces of tape.

3 Flip the case over and place three more pieces of duct tape between the cardboard pieces, aligned with the first pieces of tape. Pinch the tape together with your fingers so that the sticky sides stay together.

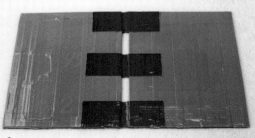

4 To make the screen frame, cut 2 of the super-strong strips to match the length of the device, and cut 2 to match the width.

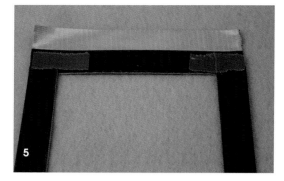

5 Line up the frame strips in the shape of the device (probably a rectangle) and place a small, thin piece of tape at each corner to hold them in place. Secure the frame by folding a standard piece of duct tape over each end.

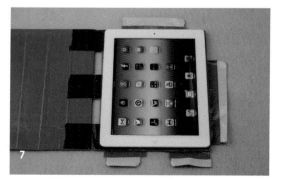

6 To make the straps that will attach to the screen frame of the cardboard-case piece, stick strips of tape lengthwise to the back of the case, with about 1/2 inch of tape sticking to the back of the case and the rest of the sticky side facing up. You don't need to add any strips of tape on the binding side of the case, since that's the opening where you'll slip your device into place.

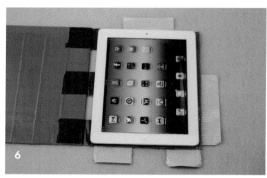

7 Seal each overhanging strip of tape with 1-inch-wide pieces of duct tape so that just about 1/2 inch of sticky tape is visible, like a sticky strip (see page 26). Use pieces of tape longer than the straps so that you can fold the ends around the backside of the straps, eliminating any sticky side bits.

8 Place your device on top of the cardboard backer and place the screen frame on top of the device. Secure the frame to the case back by pulling the straps nice and tight up and onto the frame.

9 Mark all the ports and buttons, the camera lens, etc, with a dry-erase marker. Remove your tablet from the case and cut around the marks with the X-acto knife (use extreme caution).

10 Trim any ragged bits around the frame and seal any raw edges. Use 1-inch strips of tape in the frame color to make the frame uniform and secure.

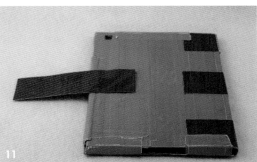

11 Now you'll make the closure strap. Place the 4-x-2-inch double-folded strip in the center of the back side of the case cover. Attach it to the case cover with strips of duct tape in the same color as the case.

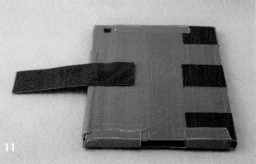

12 Trim the end of the strap to the desired shape. Place 1 piece of sticky-backed Velcro on the underside of the strap and the other piece of Velcro on front of the case. Close the strap and adhere the Velcro to the cover.

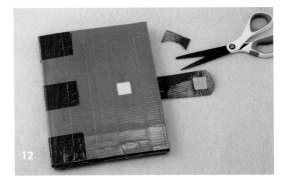

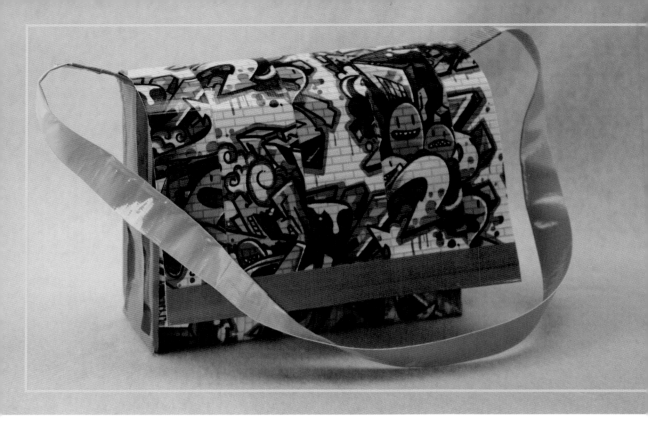

Messenger Bag

LEVEL: ● ● ● ● ● | TIME: 1 hour

MATERIALS

29-by-15-inch piece of Standard Duct Tape Fabric (page 28)

Duct tape

Scissors

Two 12-by-5-inch pieces of Standard Duct Tape Fabric

16-by-15-inch piece of Standard Duct Tape Fabric

Super-Strong Strap (see sidebar, page 136)

14 $\frac{3}{4}$-by-5 $\frac{3}{4}$-inch piece of cardboard

A messenger bag is perfect to have around in any number of situations. You can use it as an alternative to your school backpack, throw your swimsuit and towel in the pouch and head to the pool, or toss your sleepover stuff inside and take it to a friend's house. Since a messenger bag is so large, there's a lot of opportunity to use colorful tapes and embellishments. Get creative!

1 Place the 29-by-15-inch piece of duct tape fabric on the work surface. Twelve inches down from the top of this piece, place the two 12-by-5-inch pieces of duct tape fabric sticking out lengthwise from the sides of the larger piece so it looks like a plus sign. Connect the pieces with strips of duct tape.

2 Add strips of duct tape to both long sides of the extending side pieces, leaving half of the tape overhanging the edges of the fabric. The sticky side of the tape should be facing down.

3 Using the sticky strips of tape you just added to the extending side pieces, connect one of the large center pieces to the side pieces to make a half-box shape. This will be the body of the bag. The strips of tape should be on the inside of the bag. You'll cover any stickiness showing on the outside later on.

4 Use the remaining sticky-tape strips to connect the other large center piece to the opposite edges of the side pieces of fabric. Once you've made the shape of the bag, secure the outside seams with strips of duct tape to reinforce them and cover any sticky tape showing from the inside.

5 Lay the bag down and attach the 16-by-15-inch piece of duct tape fabric to the top of one side of the bag using strips of duct tape. This will be the closure flap.

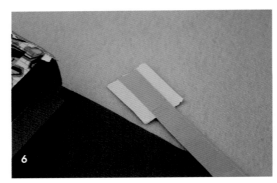

6 See the sidebar below for instructions on how to make the bag's strap. To attach the strap to the bag, place a 5-inch strip of tape on one end of the strap, forming a double-sided sticky strip.

A SUPER-STRONG STRAP

1. Connect pieces of duct tape to make one long 16-inch piece of duct tape. Flip it over and place strips of duct tape along the back of the 16-inch piece so that there's no sticky tape showing.

2. Seal the edges of the strap with 1-inch strips of duct tape folded over both the front and the back of the strap.

7 Place the bag on its side, lay the strap inside the body of the bag, and secure it to the inside of the bag. Attach the other end of the strap to the other side of the bag in the same way.

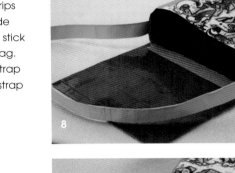

8 For extra security, place a few extra strips of tape over the end of the straps inside the bag, perpendicular to the strap. Then, stick a long strip of tape to the outside of the bag. Place the tape over the point where the strap meets the body of the bag to secure the strap even more.

9 Cover the piece of cardboard in duct tape and tape it inside the bottom of the bag to add strength and structure.

TIP!

THE RIGHT FABRIC

Easy duct tape fabric will not be strong enough for this project. Standard duct tape fabric is fine, but felt-backed or tarp-backed fabric is best.

CHAPTER

7

WEARABLE DUCT TAPE

You've already discovered that duct tape is the perfect material for folding and ripping into flat shapes, like you would use for making wallets and cases. But you can also roll, twist, braid, and stick duct tape into all kinds of combinations and shapes to make wearable duct tape accessories. Chapter 7 contains duct tape projects that will keep you decked out from head to toe in bracelets, necklaces, headbands, ties, and more! You can make these projects again and again, using different colors and patterns of tape, until you have an entire collection of duct tape accessories that's perfect for any occasion.

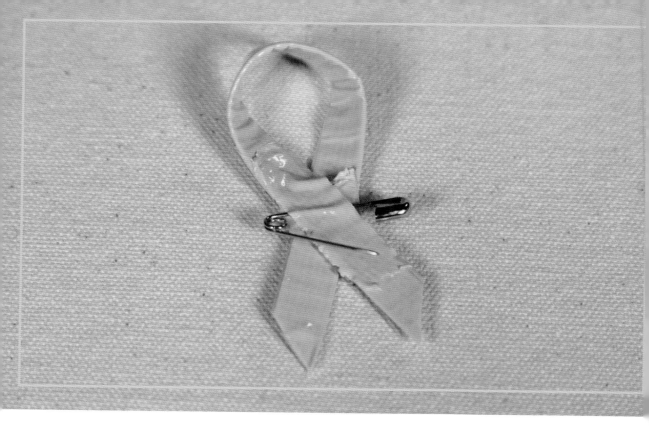

Support-Your-Cause Pin

LEVEL: ●○○○○ | TIME: 5 minutes

MATERIALS

6-by-1/2-inch
Fold-Over Strip
(page 24)

Duct tape

Scissors

Ruler

Safety pin

Bring awareness to your favorite cause with this easy-to-make pin. If you don't know what color to make your ribbon, look up your cause online. There are support-ribbon colors for almost anything, from breast cancer awareness (pink) to AIDS awareness (red) and more.

1 To make the fold-over strip into a ribbon, simply fold one side of the fold-over strip across the other and pinch it together in the middle.

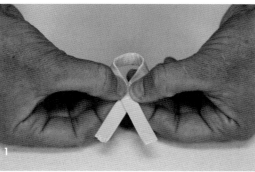

2 Cut the ends of the ribbon at an angle to make them look neat and trim.

3 Cut a piece of tape about 2 inches long and tear it into three skinny strips. Use one of the strips to wrap around the ribbon and hold it in place.

4 Now, flip the ribbon over and tape the safety pin in place with the two remaining strips of tape.

Lanyard

LEVEL: ●●○○○ ┆ TIME: 10 to 15 minutes

MATERIALS

Two 14-inch strips of duct tape

14-inch Double-Folded Strip (page 25)

Key ring

Duct tape

Scissors

L anyards are perfect for keeping keys close at hand. You can also attach a whistle, a clear pocket for your school ID, or anything else you can think of. The lanyard strap is extra strong and can be adjusted to any length you like.

1 Lay one of the 14-inch strips of duct tape sticky side up on the work surface. Place the end of the double fold-over strip in the middle of the tape, 1 inch from the end.

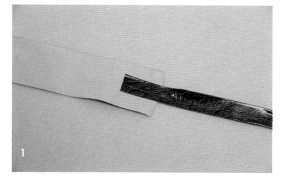

2 Fold both edges of the tape lengthwise over the double fold-over strip to seal it in place. Doing this will double the length of the strip.

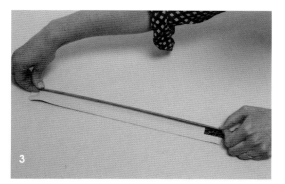

3 Repeat steps 1 and 2, folding the strip you just made inside the other 14-inch strip of duct tape. You will now have one long strip of tape.

4 Slip the key ring onto the center of the fold-over strip.

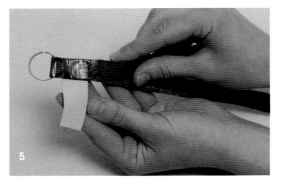

5 Pinch the sides of the fold-over strip together just above the key ring and wrap a strip of duct tape around them to secure the ring in place.

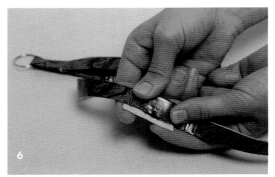

6 Secure the two loose ends of the fold-over strip with a strip of duct tape to make the lanyard into a loop. Trim any excess tape.

TIP!

SCHOOL PRIDE
If you use your lanyard to hold your school ID, choose duct tape in your school colors for an extra spirited look.

PROJECT
30

Headband

LEVEL: ● ● ○ ○ ○ ┊ TIME: 10 minutes

MATERIALS

12-inch Fold-Over
Strip (page 24)

Ruler

Scissors

Hole punch

Elastic

Stickers (page 74),
jewels, markers, etc,
for embellishing

Whether you're sliding your headband over the short tendrils of a pixie cut or a head full of long, thick locks, a headband looks great on nearly every hairstyle. It's a fun way to add some color to your look while keeping your hair out of your face at the same time. Follow these instructions to make a headband that fits your style— and your head—perfectly.

1 Start with a 12-inch fold-over strip. You can use a shorter or longer piece depending on the size of your head and how big you want your headband to be, but 12 inches is a length to start with.

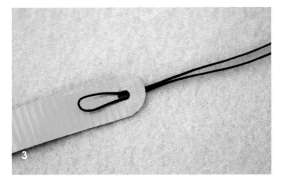

2 Use the scissors to round off the ends of the duct tape strip. Now, punch a hole in each end of the duct tape strip about $1/4$ to $1/2$ inch from the ends of the strip.

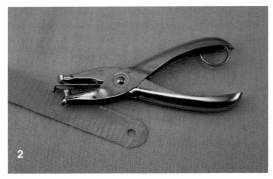

3 Next, cut a piece of elastic about 2 feet long. Fold the elastic in half and push the looped end through one of the holes in the duct tape strip.

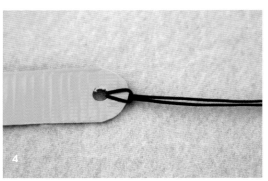

4 Feed the two loose ends of the elastic through that loop and pull gently to secure the elastic through the hole.

5 Feed the two loose elastic ends through the hole at the other end of the duct tape strip, but don't tie them off yet. Gripping the loose elastic, slide the headband onto your head and pull the elastic until it fits snugly. Hold the elastic at that point and tie it off through the open hole.

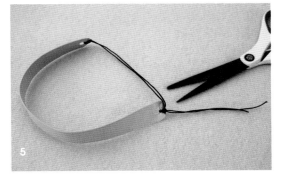

6 Your headband is finished, and now it's time to decorate! Make it sparkle and shine with stickers, jewels, cutout designs, or anything else you like.

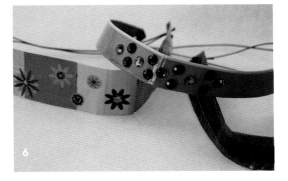

A THICKER HEADBAND

Make a thicker headband by covering the sticky side of a 12-inch piece of duct tape with smaller pieces of tape. Then, just trim the sticky edges and follow steps 2 through 6.

Beads

LEVEL: ● ○ ○ ○ ○ ┊ **TIME:** 10 to 30 minutes
(depending on the number of beads)

MATERIALS

Duct tape

Ruler

Pen

Thin strips of duct tape from $^1/_8$ to $^1/_2$ inch

Scissors

These duct tape beads are made entirely from tape. They can be cut to any size or length and used in a variety of projects. Grab your favorite color or pattern of tape and make a bunch of these beads to string on necklaces and bracelets!

1 To make a 2-inch bead, start with a 4-inch piece of duct tape. A 4-inch piece of tape will make a full loop around the pen without leaving too much overhanging tape. Fold the short end of the tape up on itself to form a sticky strip (see page 26). Place a pen at the sealed base of the sticky strip, hold it with your fingers, and roll it toward the sticky end.

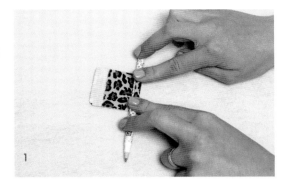

2 Roll all the way over the sticky end so that the sticky end attaches to the sealed duct tape and closes the bead.

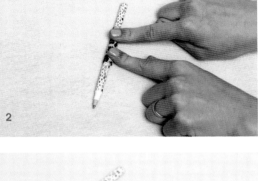

3 Embellish the beads by wrapping the thin strips of duct tape around them. When you're done embellishing, slip the beads off the pen and trim the ends so there is no stickiness showing. Trim the beads to any size you like.

MAKE A SPIRAL PATTERN

If you want to make a spiral design on your bead, start the strip of embellishing tape at an angle, with about 1 inch of tape hanging off the bead. Roll the pen in your fingers, holding the thin tape with your hand, keeping tension so that a spiral forms. Trim the ends.

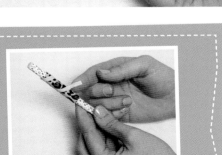

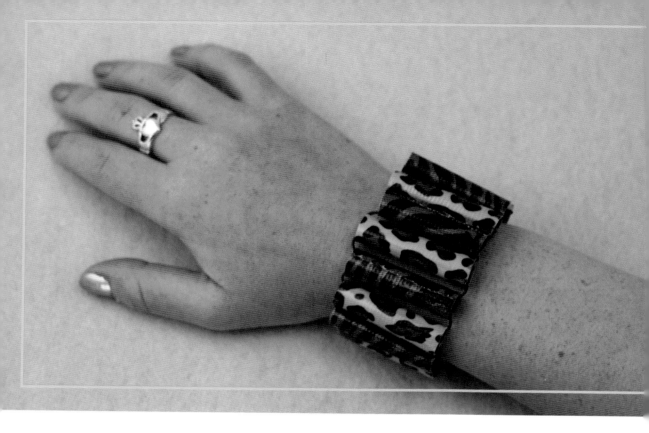

Beaded Bracelet

LEVEL: ●○○○○ ⫶ **TIME:** 10 minutes

MATERIALS

6 feet of thin beading string or elastic

Nine to fifteen 2-inch duct tape Beads (page 148)

Scissors

A beaded duct tape bracelet is a fun, three-dimensional accessory. You can also fashion this bracelet if you just can't stop making beads and need another way to use them. This project uses 2-inch duct tape beads, but you can vary the size and shape of the beads to match your own style.

1 Fold the string in half and tie a knot at the fold to make a small loop.

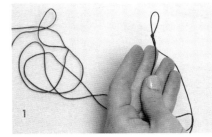

2 Hold one end of the string in your left hand and the other in your right. Feed the left-hand string through the bead from the left and the right-hand string through the bead from the right. (The two ends of the string will cross inside the bead.)

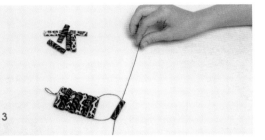

3 Continue adding beads in this way, feeding the strings through the sides.

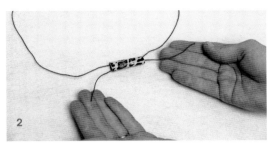

4 When you have strung enough beads to fit around your wrist, tie the string off outside the final bead. Tie the long, tied-off ends of the string through the loop you made in step 1 to secure the bracelet around your wrist. Trim any loose, hanging string.

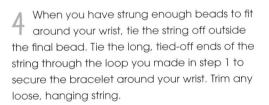

TIP!

QUICK-AND-EASY BEADS

You can make quick-and-easy beads by covering a plastic drinking straw with duct tape and cutting it to size.

Layered Jewelry

LEVEL: ● ○ ○ ○ ○ ┆ **TIME:** 10 minutes

MATERIALS

Dry-erase marker

Two 3-by-5-inch pieces of Standard Duct Tape Fabric (page 28)

Scissors

Pipe cleaner

Bead

Duct tape or a duct tape sticker

Chain, twine, ribbon, or yarn

Creating custom jewelry is a fun way to spend an afternoon and add unique flair to your jewelry collection. Once you learn the basic steps needed to create layered jewelry, you can apply them to pretty much any project. With little more than some duct tape and a great idea, you can create almost anything you want!

1 Using the dry-erase marker, draw a circle on one piece of duct tape fabric and a flower on the other. They should be about the same size so that the flower will fit nicely on the circle.

2 Cut out the shapes and fold them both in half. Carefully make two small snips ¹/2 inch apart near the center of each shape. This is where you'll attach the pieces together, so line them up the way you want them before cutting.

3 Cut the pipe cleaner in half. String a bead onto the pipe cleaner, and bend the pipe cleaner in half, using the bead as a center point. Push both legs of the pipe cleaner through the slits in your flower shape, going from front to back.

4 Now, push the pipe cleaner legs through the slits in the circle shape, going from front to back, attaching the flower and circle together.

USE UP YOUR TAPE

Save your bits and snips for these layered jewelry projects. Layered jewelry is perfect for those little bits of duct tape that you have left over from other projects.

5 Fold the pipe cleaner legs over each other to hold everything together, then trim the excess pipe cleaner. Use either a sticker or a spare piece of duct tape to firmly seal the pipe cleaner in place.

6 Using the scissors, make a tiny snip at the top of the circle shape. Loop the length of chain, twine, ribbon, or yarn through this hole, like you did for the headband (page 146, steps 3 and 4). Now you have a necklace!

MAKE A RING
To make a ring instead of a pendant, take the remainder of the pipe cleaner legs and twist them together into a ring shape instead of trimming and sealing them. Be sure that any sharp pipe cleaner ends are carefully tucked away from the skin.

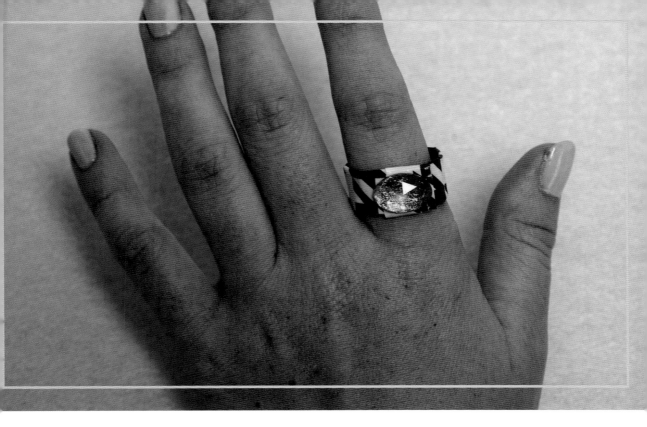

Simple Ring

LEVEL: ● ○ ○ ○ ○ | **TIME:** 10 to 15 minutes

MATERIALS

7-by-$^1/_2$-inch
Fold-Over Strip
(page 24)

Duct tape

Scissors

Parchment paper
(see sidebar)

Ruler

A duct tape ring will add a burst of color or pattern to your finger and use up some extra bits of duct tape you have left over from other projects. This ring includes directions for adding a bow, but you can add almost any embellishment you like to the ring. You can also use the techniques from this project to make a bracelet or anklet.

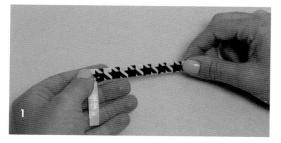

1 Cut a 1/4-inch-wide strip of duct tape and place the end at the edge of the fold-over strip.

2 Wrap the free end of the fold-over strip around your finger, and use the 1/4-inch strip of tape to secure it in place.

3 Remove the ring from your finger and trim any excess tape from the ring.

CUT STRIPS QUICKLY

Rings and small jewelry items often require tiny strips of duct tape. To make small strips of tape with clean edges, stick a piece of duct tape on a piece of parchment paper. Cut strips across the width of the duct tape. The strips will stick like stickers on the parchment paper so they can be set aside until needed.

Add a Duct Tape Bow

1 Embellish the ring however you like. If you want to embellish the ring with a tiny duct tape bow, follow steps 2 through 5.

2 To make the bow, fold a 6-inch piece of duct tape into a sticky strip (see page 26). Trim the closed end off so the strip is 2 ½ inches long.

3 Fold up the closed end onto the sticky tape and seal it to make a loop. Cut the loop in half.

4 Crease one of the loops lengthwise, then pinch it into a bow shape and secure the center with a piece of duct tape.

5 Attach the bow to the ring by placing a thin strip of duct tape across the underside of the ring base and wrapping the duct tape up and around the bow from both sides.

PROJECT 35

Spike-Rose Ring

LEVEL: ●●●○○ ⦙ TIME: 30 minutes

MATERIALS

Duct tape

Scissors

Ring-pop base

Jewels, stickers, and ribbon for embellishment (optional)

Create a brand-new accessory out of your favorite colors of duct tape with this flower-ring project. Make the flower as small or large as you want, depending on your preference. Once you master the flower technique, you can experiment with other types of designs on your ring base to create a whole handful of rings.

1 Cut about twenty or thirty 2-inch square pieces of duct tape in various colors. Make each piece into a house shape by folding in both of the top corners to meet in the center of the tape.

2 Take one duct tape house and wrap it around the base of the ring pop with its pointy side up.

3 Now, just keep wrapping more of the house pieces around that base. Alternate the placement of the point of each house to make the tape look more like the petals of a flower.

4 Once the flower is looking the way you want it to, wrap a piece of duct tape about 3 inches long by $1/2$ inch wide around the base of the ring to seal the ends in place and give it a finished look.

5 Your ring is finished! You can leave it just like this, or feel free to add some embellishments like jewels, ribbons, or colorful duct tape stickers.

PROJECT 36

Spike Bracelet

LEVEL: ●●●○○ | TIME: 30 minutes

MATERIALS

Duct tape

Scissors

Ruler (optional)

This spike bracelet has the cool look of fish scales and can be made using any patterns or colors of duct tape you choose. Try experimenting with the width of the bracelet—making a thin strip or a wide bangle—by increasing or decreasing the size of the duct tape pieces you use. Stack a bunch of these bracelets on your arm for a high-impact look, or make one simple band and wear it every day.

1. Start by tearing or cutting about thirty 2-inch square pieces of duct tape in the colors or patterns you want for your bracelet. Make each piece into a house shape by folding both of the top corners in to meet at the center of the tape.

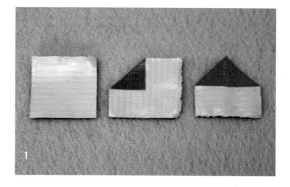

2. Lay the first house piece sticky side down on the work surface. Lay the next piece down on top of the first one. You want to line up the sides of the pieces, but leave a 1/4-inch gap from the top of the first triangle point to the second.

3. Keep overlapping house pieces until you have a long chain. At this point, you can wrap the chain around your wrist to estimate how long you need it to be. Add or remove pieces as necessary.

4. Flip the chain over so that it's sticky side up and fold both long sides in to meet each other. Don't worry if the sides don't meet exactly in the middle. You'll cover the center up with a strip of duct tape in the next step.

5 Cut another piece of duct tape about ¼ inch wide that's a little longer than the chain. Lay that strip down the center of the chain at the seam where the two folded-in sides meet. This will cover up any exposed stickiness and reinforce the bracelet. Leave some of the duct tape strip hanging off the end of the chain.

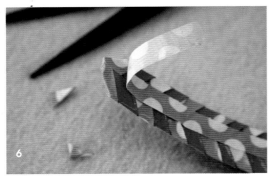

6 Snip the corners of the flat end of the chain so it comes to a point.

7 Bend the chain into a circle and insert the pointy end you cut in step 6 into the opening of the opposite end of the chain. Smooth down the center strip of duct tape so that it covers the joint. For extra reinforcement, you can take another strip of duct tape and wrap it around the joint, tucking it under the outside spikes so it doesn't affect your design.

STICKY HIGH-FIVE

Cassandra, age 10, Rhode Island
Cassandra took the idea of creating duct tape house pieces and ran with it. Her creativity inspired many duct tape projects, including this spike bracelet.

King's Crown Spike Bracelet

LEVEL: ●●○○○ ┊ TIME: 20 minutes

MATERIALS

15 duct tape "house" pieces (see page 159, step 1)

Duct tape

Scissors

Ruler

This bracelet can be made more quickly than the Spike Bracelet (page 160) because it uses fewer duct tape house pieces. Stack this King's Crown Spike Bracelet on your wrist with a lot of other duct tape bracelets for an armful of colors and patterns.

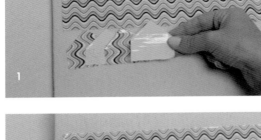

1 Cut a 12-inch strip of duct tape and lay it sticky side down on the work surface. Place one house piece right below the left edge of the tape. Lay additional house pieces out, one on top of the other. Overlap the house pieces, using the tape as your guide.

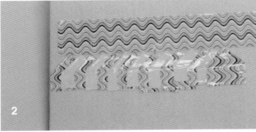

2 Continue this until the chain of house pieces is 2 inches longer than the circumference of your wrist.

3 Place the 12-inch strip of duct tape along the bottom flat edge of the house pieces, sealing them together.

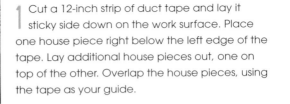

4 Flip the bracelet over and fold the guide strip up lengthwise, sealing in the bottom of the house pieces.

5 Flip the tops of the house pieces down onto the tape, sealing the sticky part to the tape.

6 Trim any excess tape from either end.

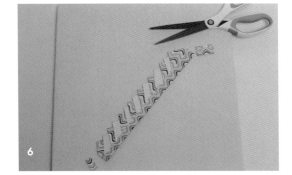

7 Place a 1-by-3-inch piece of tape on the backside of one end of the bracelet that sticks out from one of the ends.

8 Line up the two ends of your bracelet so that it joins on top of the sticky tape. Place one more house piece on top of the seam, folding the squared end over the bracelet to seal it.

9 Add a $1/4$-inch strip of tape around the outside of the bracelet to give it a finished look.

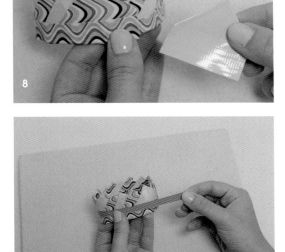

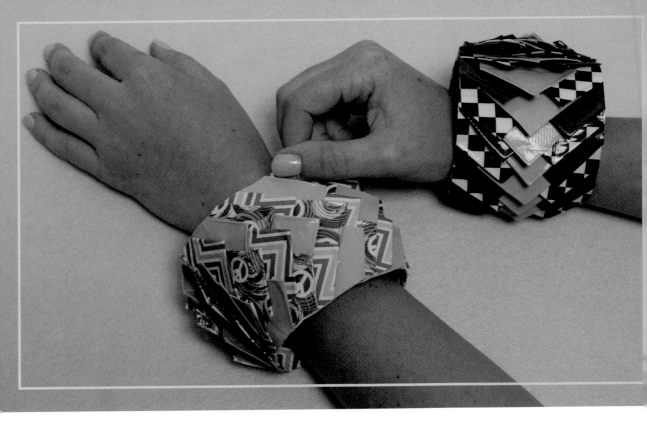

Double-Spike Bracelet

LEVEL: ●●○○○ ¦ TIME: 45 minutes

MATERIALS

60 duct tape "house" pieces (see page 159, step 1)

Ruler

Duct tape

Scissors

Like the single-spike bracelet on page 160, this project uses the technique of layering little duct tape "house" pieces. The project itself doesn't take long once the houses are made, so you can make a lot of house pieces ahead of time if you want to assemble the jewelry quickly.

1 Place two of the house pieces side by side on the work surface, overlapping their sides by about 1/2 inch.

2 Place a third house piece in the center of the first two a bit lower to fill in the space. This will be the first layer of your bracelet.

3 Repeat this pattern until you've created a bracelet that is 2 inches longer than the length needed to wrap around your wrist.

4 Flip the bracelet over and seal the back of it with two long strips of duct tape, leaving an overhang of about 2 inches of tape at the flat end of the bracelet. Trim any sticky bits overhanging the sides of the bracelet.

5 Bring the sticky end of the bracelet to meet the other, pointy house end. You may need to add one last house piece between the ending two points to finish off the pattern. Add a loop of tape, sticky side out, and seal the tape with your fingers to finish the bracelet.

Bits-and-Snips Bracelet

LEVEL: ●○○○○ | TIME: 10 to 15 minutes

MATERIALS

9-to-12-inch piece of duct tape

Little bits and snips of duct tape left over from other projects

Packing tape

Scissors

This bracelet is a great project for using up all those leftover bits and pieces from your other projects. The combination of all the various colors and patterns gives this bracelet a vibrant, modern appeal.

1 Lay the strip of duct tape on the work surface, sticky side up. Begin placing the bits and snips of tape on top of the sticky side. Don't worry if pieces hang over the edge of the tape or overlap each other; just aim to cover as much of the sticky tape as possible.

2 Place two overlapping strips of packing tape over the bits and snips, securing everything in place.

3 Flip the bracelet over and trim the packing tape and overhanging pieces of tape slightly inside the duct tape edge.

4 With the decorated side of the bracelet facing up, place a strip of packing tape sticky side up under one end of the bracelet, perpendicular to the bracelet. Size the bracelet over the widest part of your hand and secure the ends together by wrapping the tabs of packing tape around the bracelet.

TIP!

THE RIGHT SIZE

Sizing your bracelet over the widest part of your hand ensures that you'll be able to slide it easily onto your wrist.

PROJECT
40

Choker

LEVEL: ● ● ○ ○ ○ ┆ TIME: 15 minutes

MATERIALS

14-inch Double-
Folded Strip
(page 25)

Duct tape

Measuring tape

String or ribbon

3- to 4-inch Double-
Folded Strip

Scissors

Sticky-backed
Velcro (optional)

This choker design is very simple by itself. It's in the embellishments where you can really get as elaborate as you want.
To attach your embellishments, you'll add a simple slider
piece to your choker. You can also make a shorter choker and
wear it as a bracelet or anklet.

1 Fold one of the ends of the 14-inch double-folded strip back onto the strip 1 inch and secure it with a narrow strip of duct tape.

2 Measure your neck with the measuring tape. Lay the choker down on the work surface and cut the unfolded end off to match your neck measurement. Once you've trimmed off that end, repeat step 1. You will now have a loop at each end of the double-folded strip.

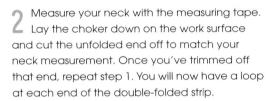

3 Now, thread the string through the loops you've made at each end of the choker. Tie off each end and trim any excess string.

4 To make the slider piece, take the 3- to 4-inch double-folded strip and place a strip of duct tape on one end. Lay this T-shaped piece of duct tape on the work surface, sticky side down, and place the choker strip across the long end so that the short end of the T is parallel to the choker strip.

5 Now, fold the short side of the T backward over the choker strip so that it is still parallel to the choker strip and the long side of the T wraps around the choker strip in a loop.

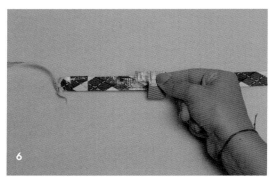

6 Fold the long side of the T up and over the choker. Leave a little bit of extra room so you can attach your embellishments to the slider piece.

7 Now the slider piece is a loop that can slide on and off the choker. Slide it off the choker strip and fold the short sticky parts of the T shape around the slider piece to secure it. Trim any excess tape.

8 To add an embellishment to the slider piece, slip a small strip of tape through the loop of the slider piece, and attach your embellishment to that piece of tape.

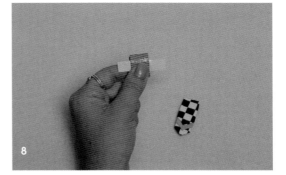

9 Slip the slider piece with embellishment over one end of the choker, and tie the end of the string around your neck to fit.

MAKE A VELCRO CLOSURE

You can use Velcro for the closure instead of string or ribbon. Just make the choker strip about 2 inches longer than you would for a choker with a string closure, and add sticky-backed Velcro on the ends instead of loops for string. Make sure you add one piece of Velcro to the inside of the strip and one to the outside so they close without twisting the choker.

Tie

LEVEL: ● ● ● ○ ○ ⋮ **TIME: 45 minutes**

MATERIALS

Duct tape

Scissors

Dry-erase marker

Ruler

Choker sized to fit around the collar of a shirt (see page 170)

Another creative accessory for the duct tape prom—or even just for everyday wear—is a duct tape tie. Duct tape comes in so many colors and patterns that some of them actually mimic the look of real fabric. A black duct tape tie can easily take on the look of leather, while a paisley- or gingham-print tie will fit right in at a picnic or garden party.

1 Cut a strip of duct tape 2 inches longer than the length you want the completed tie to be. For instance, if you want a 14-inch tie, cut a 16-inch strip of tape. Place the strip sticky side down on the work surface.

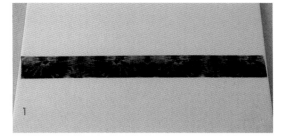

2 With the dry-erase marker, mark the center of the short end of the tape. Fold the tape up 2 inches on that end, sticky side out.

3 Using the center mark as a guide, fold down the corners on the end you just folded to make a triangle point.

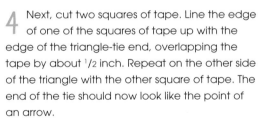

4 Next, cut two squares of tape. Line the edge of one of the squares of tape up with the edge of the triangle-tie end, overlapping the tape by about 1/2 inch. Repeat on the other side of the triangle with the other square of tape. The end of the tie should now look like the point of an arrow.

5 Decide how wide you want the tie to be and use the ruler to measure out the width. Make marks on the squares you attached to use as guides for the width. For our tie, we chose a 3-inch width.

6 Now, you'll add strips of duct tape to make the length of the tie the correct width. Attach a strip of duct tape down the length of the tie; repeat on the other side until it is the desired width.

7 Flip the tie over so the sticky side faces up. Fold in the tiny corner pieces overhanging the end of the tie and adhere them to the sticky side.

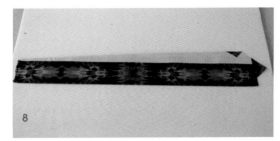

8 Cover the sticky side of the tie with strips of duct tape, leaving about 1 inch of sticky tape visible at the square end. Try to use as few strips of tape as possible, keeping them long and wide to preserve the pattern of the tie. Let the square ends of the tape overhang the triangular end of the tie. This will be the front of the tie.

9 Flip the tie over and fold up the overhanging bits of sticky tape. Trim any unfinished edges.

TIP!

MIX AND MATCH
You can make different kinds of ties to slide on and off the same choker piece.

10 With the back of the tie facing up, fold the sticky strip at the top of the tie down about 2 inches to form a loop. Secure the loop with a matching piece of tape.

11 Flip the tie over to its front and lay a strip of duct tape sideways across the top of the tie, just under the loop. The tape should hang over each side of the tie by about 1 1/2 inches. Flip the tie back over and fold both overhanging edges of tape in at an angle to make the knot for the tie. Try different angles to make varying knots, if you like.

12 Now, detach the loop and place another strip of tape the same length as the strip from step 11 directly above that strip overlapping by 1/4 inch. Fold the edges in the same way so that it forms a triangle with the other strip. Fold the triangles in until they are flush with the edge of the tie and secure them with a piece of tape.

13 Fold the "knot" down and resecure the sticky tape. Add another strip of tape to secure it in place. Slip the tie onto the choker. Embellish the tie any way you want.

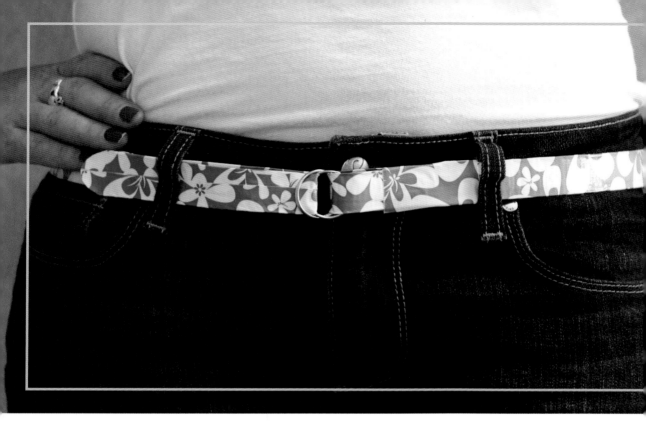

PROJECT
42

Belt

LEVEL: ●●○○○ ⁞ TIME: 20 minutes

MATERIALS

String or yarn
Duct tape
Scissors
2 key rings

A belt is an essential wardrobe staple. For one thing, it keeps your pants up! It also adds a nice pop of color to your outfit. Make belts from all your favorite colors and patterns of duct tape to spice up your wardrobe.

1 Determine the length of the belt by measuring a belt you already own or by wrapping a piece of string or yarn around your waist. (Make sure you leave plenty of extra string to account for the overlapping end of the belt.)

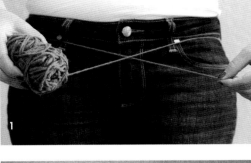

2 Measure out a strip of duct tape the length of the string. Fold it on itself lengthwise in thirds so that there's no sticky tape showing (see the double-folded strip on page 25).

3 Stack the 2 key rings and slide them onto one end of the duct tape strip. Fold the end of the strip over onto itself, trapping the rings inside the bend. With another piece of duct tape, tape this fold shut, securing the rings.

4 Trim the other end of the belt into the desired shape. To secure the belt around your waist, thread the free end through the two rings, then bend it back and through the second ring and gently tug it tight.

CHAPTER

8

AT SCHOOL

Standard school supplies are often pretty basic and boring. Take your school supplies to the next level by making them out of duct tape! The projects in Chapter 8 will show you how to make your own duct tape supplies that are both functional and fabulous. From simple projects like the Pencil Case (page 190) to more complex endeavors like the Backpack (page 204), you can head to school in style with a little bit of help from your roll.

Bookmark with Tassel

LEVEL: ● ○ ○ ○ ○ ┆ TIME: 10 minutes

MATERIALS

2-by-6-inch piece of Standard Duct Tape Fabric (page 28)

Scissors

Hole punch

4-by-¹/₄-inch Fold-Over Strip (page 24)

Tassel with loop (page 50)

Duct tape

A bookmark with a tassel is one simple way to use the end of the duct tape roll. You can make the bookmark base out of a strip of duct tape from the end of a roll, and a tassel is easy to make out of leftover duct tape pieces. Slide the bookmark inside your favorite book, and you're good to go!

1 Trim the ends of the duct tape fabric to the shapes you want. This will be your bookmark.

2 Punch a hole in the top of the bookmark at least $3/4$ inch down from the edge.

3 Slide the $1/4$-inch fold-over strip through the hole, through the loop of the tassel, and back through the hole in the bookmark to make a circle. Use a small piece of tape to secure the overlap. Trim any excess tape.

Luggage Tag

LEVEL: ●●○○○ | TIME: 15 minutes

MATERIALS

2 1/2-by-4-inch
Clear Window
(page 34)

Duct tape

4 1/2-by-3-inch
piece of Standard
Duct Tape Fabric
(page 28)

Scissors

10-inch 3-fold
strip (see sidebar,
page 25)

Two 2-inch 4-fold
strips (see sidebar,
page 25)

Paper for informa-
tion card

Great for a trip or just marking your belong-ings, this luggage tag is quick and easy to make but surprisingly durable. The double-lock tongue closure makes it easy to take on and off and switch to a backpack or purse. For extra security, you can add an additional strip of tape to the closure once the tag is in place.

1 Seal one end of the window by placing a
  ¹/₂-inch strip of duct tape half on, half off the
edge of the window.

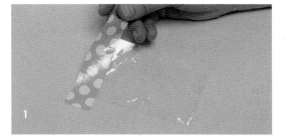

2 Fold the strip over to form a duct tape end
  to the window and trim any overhanging bits
of tape. This will be where your info card slides in
and out of the window.

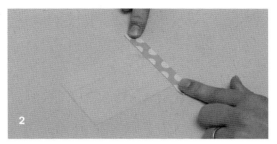

3 Center the window on the duct tape fabric
  and secure the other three sides in place
with strips of duct tape. Wrap half of the tape
lengthwise around the back of the fabric for a
clean border. Make sure you leave the end of
the window where your information card slides in
and out unsealed. Trim off any excess tape.

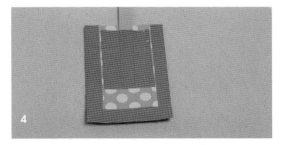

4 Flip the tag over and center the 3-fold strip
  on the back. Secure the strip with tape at
least 1 ¹/₂ to 2 inches down the strip for maxi-
mum hold.

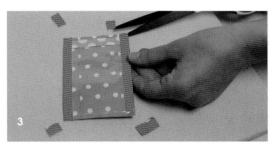

COLORFUL CLOSURE

To add more color to the closure,
make the thin fold-over strips out
of a different color or pattern of
duct tape than the thicker strip.

5 Lay the two 4-fold strips directly on top of the taped strap as you would for a double-tongue closure (see page 40).

6 Secure the 4-fold strips with tape on either side. These strips will lock the luggage-tag strap in place.

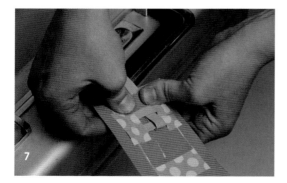

7 Slip the luggage-tag strap through the luggage handle and slide the strap down through the two locking strips, then back up through the top locking strip.

8 Slip your information card inside the tag window.

PROJECT
45

Locker Organizer

LEVEL: ●●●○ ¦ TIME: 60 minutes

MATERIALS

Shoebox lid

Duct tape

Scissors

Corks (for the bulletin board)

Hot-glue gun

Plastic water bottle (for the pencil cup)

Small box, such as a mini cereal box

Wire clothes hanger

Wire cutters

Sticky-backed magnet strips (optional)

Your locker is a place to keep your books, notes, gym clothes, and more. But it's not always the best place to keep things organized. That's where this locker organizer comes in. Express your personal style by using your favorite colors and patterns of duct tape and prepare yourself for a lot of compliments every time you open your locker door.

1 Line the inside of the shoebox lid with duct tape. Then, wrap strips of duct tape around the outside of the rim of the shoebox lid and fold them down into the lid to cover the outside and the inside rim.

2 Now that the box lid is lined with tape, it's time to place the corkboard. Carefully hot-glue corks into the box lid in the arrangement you like. You can cover the whole lid with corks, or just a small section.

3 Next, add the pencil cup and a small box to hold odds and ends. To make the pencil cup, carefully cut the top off a plastic water bottle so you're left with the flat bottle base. To make the small box, cut the lid off a mini cereal box or another small box so that it has an open top. Cover the bottle base and box with duct tape.

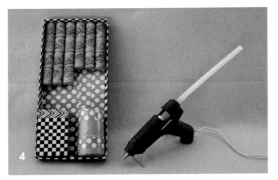

4 Attach the cup and box to the inside of the box lid with hot glue.

5 Now you can hang the locker organizer in your locker and fill it with your stuff. Use the hook part of a wire hanger to hang the organizer. Hold the wire hanger up to the back of the organizer to estimate how much of the hanger you'll need to cut off, and trim the hanger to size with the wire cutters.

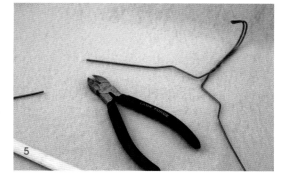

6 Twist the hook part of the hanger about 45 degrees so that the hook faces the direction you need to hang the organizer. Affix the hanger to the back of the organizer with strips of duct tape.

TRY MAGNETS INSTEAD

Another way to attach your locker organizer to your locker is with magnets. Get some sticky-backed magnet strips and stick them to the back of your shoebox lid. You'll probably want to cover the whole back of the lid in order to support your organizer and everything inside it.

Pencil Case

LEVEL: ●●○○○ ┆ **TIME:** 20 minutes

MATERIALS

Ziploc bag
(heavy-duty
one-gallon size)

Three-ring binder
for measuring

Duct tape

Scissors

Dry-erase marker

Hole punch

A pencil case is a handy spot to hold your pencils (obviously), pens, erasers, scissors, staples, and more. This duct tape pencil case clips into your binder, ensuring that you'll always have your supplies when you need them.

1 Line up the bottom of the Ziploc bag with the rings of the binder. The top of the bag will extend past the top of the binder. Fold the bottom of the bag up onto itself to make the pouch fit inside the binder.

2 Secure the folded flap of the bag with a strip of duct tape. The tape should be slightly longer than the bag, with a few inches overhanging on the sides. Wrap the overhanging ends of tape around to the back of the bag and secure them in place.

3 Continue covering the bag with strips of duct tape. All the strips should hang over the sides of the bag but not over the Ziploc top.

4 Flip the bag over and fold over the overhanging tape onto the back. Cover the rest of the bag with strips of duct tape. Trim any overhanging pieces of tape, but be careful not to cut into the bag itself.

5 Line up the bottom of the bag with the binder's rings. Using a dry-erase marker, mark where you should punch the holes for the binder's rings about $1/2$ inch in from each edge, then punch through the bag with the hole punch.

6 Decorate the pencil case with more duct tape, stickers, or anything else you choose.

STAY ORGANIZED

Make a pencil case to hold your loose duct tape crafting supplies (such as scissors, dry-erase markers, and hole punchers) and stick it in your portable workstation.

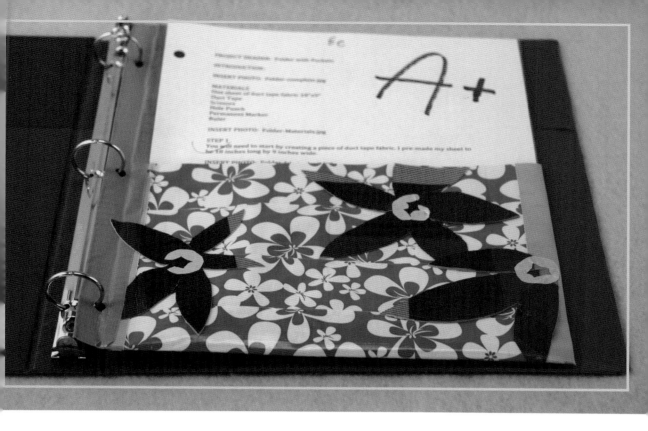

Folder with Pockets

LEVEL: ●●○○○ | TIME: 30 minutes

MATERIALS

18-by-9 ¹/₂-inch piece of Standard Duct Tape Fabric (page 28)

Ruler

Piece of notebook paper for measuring

Duct tape

Scissors

Binder for measuring

Dry-erase marker

Hole punch

Keep your homework and class notes organized in this duct tape folder. You can slip a few of these folders in your binder to colorfully categorize your papers, or keep them loose in your backpack in case of a paper emergency. Decorate your folders however you like, adding stickers, tassels, or any other embellishments you choose.

1 Create a pocket in the duct tape fabric by folding the short side of the fabric up onto itself about 6 inches. This pocket will hold your papers, so slide a piece of notebook paper inside the fold to make sure that the folder will be tall enough. Create a crease at the fold.

2 Seal the edges of the pocket with strips of duct tape the same length as the height of the pocket.

3 Now, tear some more duct tape strips and seal the other edges of the duct tape fabric to strengthen them. Don't seal the pocket closed, but wrap the strips around the outside folder edges to reinforce them. Trim any excess tape. For added strength, add two layers of duct tape to the side of the folder that will clip into the binder.

4 Lay the folder inside the binder and mark the spots where you should punch the holes for the binder rings with a dry-erase marker about 1/2 inch in from the edge. Punch holes where you have marked.

5 Embellish and decorate the folder as you like.

A TWO-POCKET FOLDER

To make a 2-pocket folder, simply lay two 1-pocket folders side by side with 1/4 inch of space between them. Then connect them with strips of tape.

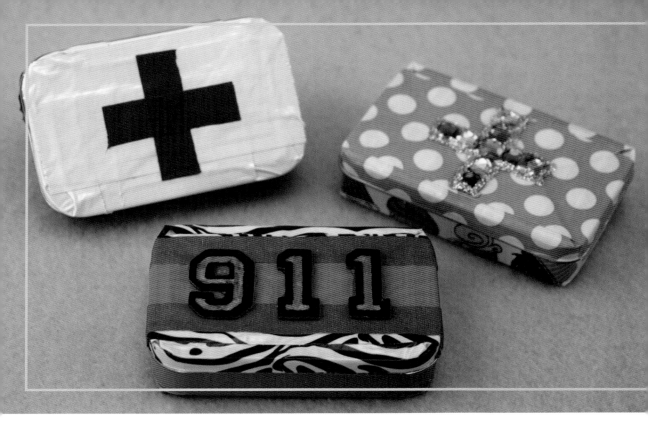

Altoid Tin First-Aid Kit

LEVEL: ●●○○○ ⋮ TIME: 20 minutes

MATERIALS

Duct tape

Scissors

Empty Altoid tin or similar box

Duct tape stickers and other decorations

Bandages, tweezers, pain-relief medication, and other first-aid supplies

Embellishments (optional)

Y ou never know when you might get a blister, a splinter, or maybe just a headache. With this handy first-aid kit, you'll be prepared for any minor injury or pain and be able to help your friends out, too. You can also use the techniques in this project to make any kind of decorative box to hold any number of items.

1 Start with a clean, empty Altoid tin. Tear off a strip of duct tape long enough to go around the perimeter of the tin, and wrap it around the outside of the lid. Make sure you don't tape the lid shut.

2 Fold the tape down to cover the lid of the box. If it doesn't reach all the way to the middle, cover any parts of the box that show with another piece of duct tape.

3 Flip the tin over and repeat steps 1 and 2 on the base of the tin.

4 Decorate the tin however you like and fill it with first-aid supplies.

TIP!

TRIM THE CORNERS

Before you fold the tape down onto the lid, use the scissors to cut small slits in the tape at the corners. This will make it much easier to fold the edges down neatly.

Book Cover

LEVEL: ●●○○○ ⦙ TIME: 20 minutes

MATERIALS

Book for measuring

Ruler or tape measure

Standard Duct Tape Fabric in desired size (page 28)

Duct tape

Dry-erase marker

Scissors

This removable book cover is perfect for personalizing schoolbooks and journals. Many schools require textbooks to be covered, so why not make a durable, colorful cover out of duct tape instead of cutting up yet another grocery bag? To help protect your favorite novel from bumps and bruises during your travels, you can also make a book cover for it before going on a trip.

1 First, you need to measure your book to determine how big to make the duct tape fabric. Measure the length of the book and add $1/4$ inch to get the length of the duct tape fabric. (The book we're using is $6\,1/2$ inches long, so our fabric will be $6\,3/4$ inches long.)

2 Now, measure the width of the book, add 1 inch to that measurement, and multiply that number by 3 to get the width of the duct tape fabric. For the book we're using, the book's width is $4\,1/2$ inches. Add 1 inch = $5\,1/2$ inches. Multiply $5\,1/2$ by 3 = $16\,1/2$ inches.

3 Make a piece of standard duct tape fabric (see page 28) according to the measurements you got in steps 1 and 2. For the book we're using, the fabric will be $6\,3/4$ x $16\,1/2$ inches.

4 Place the book's spine in the center of the duct tape fabric and use the dry-erase marker to mark where the edge of the open book lies.

5 Remove the book and fold the edge of the fabric to that mark to make a flap. Secure the flap on either side with strips of tape to make it into a pocket.

6 Open the book and slip the front cover into the flap, then use the dry-erase marker to mark where the back cover of the book lies on the fabric.

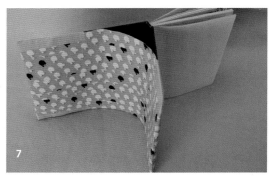

7 Remove the book and repeat step 5 with the back flap of the book cover. To put the book cover on your book, open the book up as far as the spine will allow. Slip the front and back covers into the flaps and close the book.

Lunch Bag

LEVEL: ● ● ● ○ ○ ⁞ **TIME: 45 to 60 minutes**

MATERIALS

Two 7-by-12-inch pieces of Ziploc Closure fabric (page 44)

Two 4-by-12-inch pieces of Standard Duct Tape Fabric (page 28)

4-by-7-inch piece of Standard Duct Tape Fabric

Duct tape

Dry-erase marker

Ruler

Scissors

It's a waste to use a different paper bag to carry your lunch every day. Make this duct tape lunch bag so your peanut butter sandwich can ride to school in style. This bag is durable and spill-proof and can easily be rinsed out before you use it again.

1 Lay the pieces of Ziploc closure fabric and duct tape fabric out on the work surface in this order: Ziploc fabric, 4-by-12-inch duct tape fabric, Ziploc fabric, 4-by-12-inch duct tape fabric. Now, move the two 4-by-12-inch pieces of duct tape fabric down $1/2$ inch so that the short edges of the Ziploc fabric stick out higher than their short edges do.

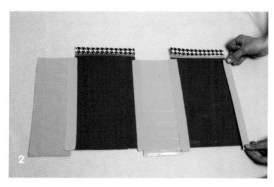

2 Use 1-inch strips of tape to secure the long sides of the fabric pieces together. Add an additional strip of tape at one end, leaving half of the sticky side hanging over the edge of the fabric.

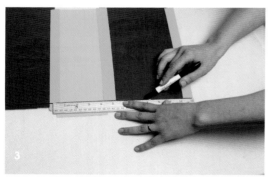

3 Use a ruler to make a straight line along the bottom of the pieces of fabric and trim along this line.

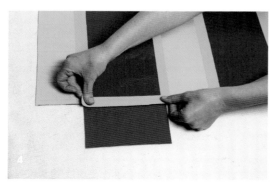

4 Place the remaining piece of duct tape fabric at the bottom of the center piece of Ziploc fabric and attach it with a strip of duct tape.

5 Flip the bag over and place a 1-inch strip of duct tape across the top of all the pieces of fabric to connect them. Make sure the piece of connector tape goes below the Ziploc closures so they stick up above it. Seal the connected sticky seams with strips of duct tape.

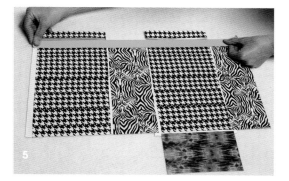

6 Fold the sides of the bag in and seal it into a bag shape with the overhanging piece of sticky tape along one side.

7 Now, finish attaching the bottom of the bag to the other sides with strips of tape. Seal any exposed sticky seams inside the bag with strips of tape.

8 Reinforce the bottom of the bag by taking a 2-inch strip of tape and wrapping it entirely around the bottom of the bag. Cut snips in each corner of the wrapped tape (see tip on page 197), and fold the tape down onto the bottom of the bag to seal it in place.

Backpack

LEVEL: ● ● ● ● ● | TIME: 2 hours

MATERIALS

Three 12-by-15-inch pieces of Standard Duct Tape Fabric (page 28)

Dry-erase marker

X-acto knife

Ruler

Two 46-inch-long, 1-inch-wide Super-Strong Strips (page 25)

Duct tape

Two 5-by-15-inch pieces of Standard Duct Tape Fabric

5-by-12-inch piece of Standard Duct Tape Fabric

Hole punch

Scissors

Two 24-inch pieces of heavy cord or string

4 small key rings

Sticky-backed Velcro

Fill this backpack with school supplies, camping gear, or as many rolls of duct tape as you can fit! The structure of the backpack is basically a combination of two other projects: the Lunch Bag (page 201) and the Messenger Bag (page 134). Your backpack will need to be strong, so make sure you seal all joining edges as thoroughly as possible to ensure that the bag holds together well.

1 Place one of the 12-by-15-inch pieces of duct tape fabric on the work surface right side down. Measure 2 inches in from both 12-inch sides of the fabric and make lines there. Now, measure 2 inches in from each side on both 15-inch edges of the fabric and make a mark where the 2-inch measurement intersects with the drawn lines.

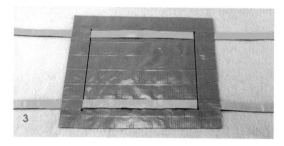

2 Using the X-acto knife, make a 1-inch slit at each of the four marks, using the line you drew as a guide (use extreme caution). Make sure you cut in toward the center of the fabric and not out toward the edges.

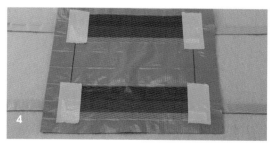

3 Now, attach the superstrong strips, which will become the backpack straps. Slide the first strap up through one of the bottom slits you made in step 2 and down through the top slit. Repeat with the other strap so you have two parallel straps.

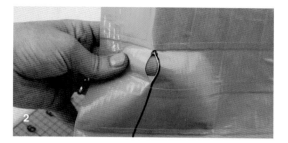

4 Secure the straps and the slits with a generous amount of duct tape. You really want to make sure they stay in place.

5 Place the pieces of duct tape fabric on the work surface in this order: 5-by-15-inch piece of fabric, 12-by-15-inch piece of fabric with straps, 5-by-15-inch piece of fabric, and 12-x-15-inch piece of fabric, leaving 1/4 inch space between each piece. Tape the pieces of fabric together with strips of duct tape.

6 Line the 5-by-12-inch piece of fabric up along the bottom of the strapless 12-by-15-inch piece of fabric and secure them together with strips of duct tape.

7 Now, fold the sides of the backpack into place. Fold the outside edge of the 5-by-15-inch piece of duct tape fabric over to meet the edge of the strapless 12-by-15-inch piece of duct tape fabric. Lay the back pack on the work surface and seal all of the seams with strips of duct tape, like you did for the lunch bag (page 201).

8 Place strips of tape along all three sides of the bottom flap, overhanging the edges by about 1/2 inch.

9 Open up the backpack and place it upside down on the work surface. Line up the bottom flap with the three remaining sides and tape it in place.

10 Secure all the seams inside the backpack with strips of tape so there is no sticky tape at any joint.

11 The remaining piece of 12-by-15-inch fabric will become the closure flap. Trim the end of the fabric to the desired flap shape. Lay the bag on its back and attach the flap with strips of duct tape, just like you've connected all the other pieces of duct tape fabric.

12 Squeeze the front and back panels of the backpack together in their upper corners to form a valley fold in each side panel. Use a hole punch to make holes on either side of the valley fold. Punch holes 1 1/2 inches in from each side on the front and back panels so you have eight holes total.

13 Tie a large knot at one end of one of the pieces of cord. Thread the other end through one of the front holes, the two side holes, the two back holes, the other two side holes, and out the other front hole. Now, tie a knot in this end to keep the cord from slipping out. Tighten the two ends of the cord to keep the backpack shut.

14 Now, add adjuster rings to the backpack straps. Slide two stacked key rings onto the end of one strap and fold the strap up and over the rings so that the strap overlaps itself by at least 2 inches. Secure this overlap by wrapping a strip of duct tape around the strap. Repeat with the other strap. Adjust the straps the same way you adjust the belt on page 178.

15 For extra security, add a piece of sticky-backed Velcro to the closure flap. Attach one side of the Velcro to the flap, then fold the flap down onto the front of the backpack and run your fingers over the Velcro to stick it in place on the front of the bag.

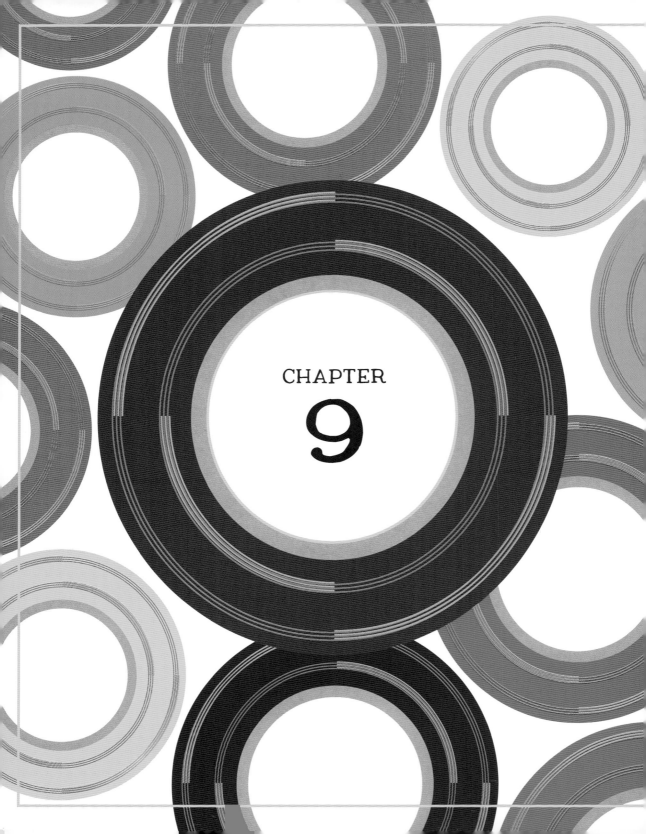

CHAPTER

9

IN YOUR ROOM

Your bedroom is your sanctuary. It's the place where you feel most comfortable, and where you can show off your personal style and express yourself through your decor. The projects in Chapter 9 will help you use your favorite colors and patterns of duct tape to add some flair to your space. Adapt the projects in this chapter to fit your needs and express your style in any way you like!

PROJECT
52

Desk Organizer

LEVEL: ●●○○○ | TIME: 30 minutes

MATERIALS

6 cardboard duct
tape roll centers

Hot-glue gun

Duct tape

One 9-by-9-inch
cardboard square

Permanent marker

Scissors

The fun doesn't have to end when you get to the end of
the duct tape roll. Make this desktop organizer out of the
cardboard duct tape roll centers and decorate it in any
way you choose. Now, that's using every last bit of the roll!

1 Stack three of the cardboard centers on top of each other and glue them together to make a 6-inch-tall tube. Then, stack and glue two cardboard centers together to make a 4-inch-tall tube. Leave the remaining cardboard center as is.

2 For extra security, wrap a thin strip of duct tape around the joints where you glued the cardboard centers together.

3 Decorate the tubes in the style you want, then place them on top of the cardboard square in the arrangement you would like them to sit on your desk.

4 Trace around the tubes on the cardboard square, cut out the shape of the tube arrangement, and glue the three tubes onto the cardboard base.

Dry-Erase Board

PROJECT 53

LEVEL: ●○○○○ | TIME: 15 minutes

MATERIALS

Corrugated cardboard

Light-colored duct tape (for white-board surface)

Duct tape in any color

Clear packing tape

Three 5-inch 3-fold strips (see sidebar, page 25)

Scissors

Dry-erase marker

Sticky-backed magnets (optional)

A dry-erase board is a handy place to write notes, reminders, grocery lists, or anything else you don't want to forget. You can customize this dry-erase board to fit whatever space you plan to put it in. Make it larger for your bedroom or small enough to fit in your locker.

1 Cut the cardboard to the desired finished whiteboard dimensions and cover it with the light-colored tape.

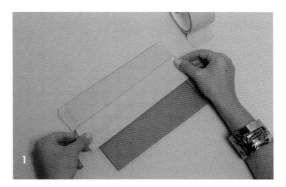

2 Now, cover one side of the board with a layer of clear packing tape. Try to make as few overlaps as possible when laying the tape so it'll be easier to write on.

3 Make a frame around the board by placing a 1-inch strip of duct tape along each edge and folding the tape over to the back of the board, wrapping the edges. Trim any excess overlapping tape.

4 Next, you'll make a holder for the dry-erase pen. Tape one end of one of the 3-fold strips to the bottom corner of the board and slip the pen under it.

5 Use your finger to press the strip into a loop large enough for the pen to fit inside, but not so loose that it will slip out. Secure the loop with tape and trim off any excess strip.

6 Twist the other two 3-fold strips into loops like you did for the Support-Your-Cause Pin ribbon (page 140).

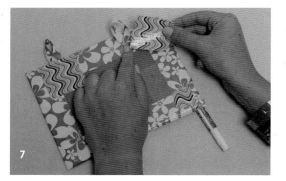

7 Tape these loops to the back of the board to use as hangers. Now you can hang the board from tacks anywhere.

MAKE IT MAGNETIC

To mount the board somewhere magnetic, like in your locker or on the refrigerator, place magnets on the back of the board instead of loops of tape.

Checkerboard

LEVEL: ● ● ● ○ ○ ┊ TIME: 35 to 40 minutes

MATERIALS

Eight 10-inch Fold-Over Strips in one color (page 24)

Duct tape

Eight 10-inch Fold-Over Strips in another color

2 cardboard-backed strips of duct tape from the end of the roll (or 2 pieces of Standard Duct Tape Fabric, page 28)

Dry-erase marker

Quarter

Scissors

This checkerboard is the perfect portable game board—just roll it up and take it on the road! Game pieces can be made from the paper-backed tape at the end of the roll, but buttons, coins, and tiny toys work, too. You can also use the techniques you learn in this project to make a place mat.

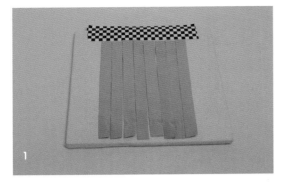

Make the Checkerboard

1 Lay eight of the same-colored fold-over strips side by side on the work surface with their long sides touching but not overlapping. Lay a strip of duct tape about 10 inches long across the top of the pieces of tape, covering about 1 inch of the top of the strips.

2 Using the fold-over strips in the other color, begin weaving the checkerboard like you would weave a piece of woven duct tape fabric (see page 32). Make sure the weaving strips stick out from the hanging strips by about 1 inch so you'll have even checkerboard squares.

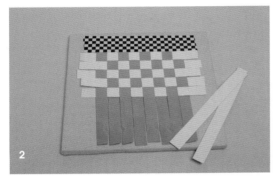

3 Once you're done weaving all the strips of tape, seal the other three sides of the checkerboard with tape like you did along the top. When you seal the sides, make sure the checkerboard squares along the edges of the board are the same size as the other squares, and not any smaller.

4 Flip the checkerboard over and fold the side pieces of tape over to seal the sides in. Cover any sticky bits of tape and trim any overhanging edges.

Make the Game Pieces

1 Use a quarter to trace 12 circles on each piece of cardboard-backed duct tape.

2 Cut out the circles and use them as checkers on the checkerboard.

TIP!

READY TO PLAY
Make an extra set of game pieces, stick them in a duct tape pouch, and toss the pouch in your Checkerboard Beach Bag (page 119) to play checkers on the go anytime.

Woven Basket

LEVEL: ●●●○ ⋮ TIME: 90 minutes

MATERIALS

Four 6-by-6-inch pieces of Woven Duct Tape Fabric (page 32)

6-by-6-inch piece of Standard Duct Tape Fabric (page 28)

Small box (optional)

Duct tape

Scissors

Hole punch

Brads

You can use a woven basket for more than just carrying your Easter eggs. Plop a woven basket next to your front door and keep your keys in it. Or set a woven basket on your desk to hold all your paper clips, Post-it Notes, and other supplies. You can even put a birthday gift in a woven basket and add some tissue paper to make the gift really special (and useful!).

1 Arrange the 4 woven pieces of fabric in a cross pattern around the 6-by-6-inch piece of standard duct tape fabric, right sides facing down. Take strips of duct tape and attach the woven fabric pieces to the sides of the center duct tape fabric square. Flip the whole thing over and do the same on the other side.

2 Create the corners of the basket by folding the woven fabric pieces up and taping the sides together. They should stand up at a 90-degree angle from the center square. You might need to use a small box or other object to help hold the center square down and make it easier to create corners. Reinforce these seams with more tape on the inside of the basket.

3 For the handle, take a long strip of duct tape and fold it over on itself lengthwise to create a long fold-over strip. If you want a wider handle, stick two pieces of duct tape together length-wise and fold them over. Use the scissors to round the ends of the strip, and use the hole punch to make holes in both ends.

4 Decide where you want to attach the handle to the sides of the basket and punch holes in each of the sides with the hole punch. Line up the holes in the basket with the holes in the handle and run a brad through both to attach them.

STICKY HIGH-FIVE

Caitlyn, age 11, Tennessee
Caitlyn used woven duct tape fabric to make an easy basket. Follow Caitlin's lead and create pillows, bags, and projects out of woven duct tape fabric.

Picture Frame

LEVEL: ● ● ○ ○ ○ | **TIME:** 30 minutes

MATERIALS

Photograph for measuring

Two pieces of corrugated cardboard, at least 1 inch larger than your photo on all sides

Pen or permanent marker

Duct tape

Ruler

X-acto knife

Self-healing mat or cutting board

Small strip of corrugated cardboard

Scissors

Embelishments (optional), see step 10

You probably have tons of pictures of your family, friends, pets, and special memories. Why not display them in some colorful duct tape frames? This frame can be customized to fit any picture, which makes it really handy for those photos or collages that don't fit in a standard frame.

1 Measure the photograph you want to frame and add 1 inch to each side's measurement. Cut the two cardboard pieces to that size. Now, take one of the pieces of cardboard and mark $3/4$ inch in from each edge with the pen to make a border.

2 Place a strip of tape along one side of the cardboard with a border, aligned with the $3/4$-inch mark.

3 Fold the tape around the back of the cardboard and trim any excess.

4 Line up three more strips of tape on the other sides, but don't fold them over.

5 With the project on the self-healing mat, place the edge of the ruler along the line of the duct tape and use the X-acto knife to cut out the inner rectangle of cardboard from the duct tape frame (use extreme caution).

6 Seal the inner frame edges you just cut with thin strips of duct tape.

7 Flip the project over and place the second large piece of cardboard directly on top of the cutout frame and use the three pieces of overlapping duct tape to connect this piece to the back of the frame. You will have one open end of the frame where you can slide photos in and out.

8 Now, make the frame's stand. Secure the smaller strip of cardboard to the back of the frame with a piece of tape, below the top.

9 Now, flip the stand up and over and place a second piece of tape on the underside of the stand.

10 Flip the frame over, slide your picture inside, and embellish the frame however you like.

TIP!

FRAME SIZES
Vary the widths of your picture frames' edges to make your collection more colorful and dynamic.

Jewelry Stand

LEVEL: ●●●○○ | **TIME:** 30 to 45 minutes

MATERIALS

Cardboard toilet paper tube

Bottle cap or other disk that will fit snugly inside the toilet paper tube

Duct tape

Hot-glue gun

Compact disc

Cardboard paper towel tube

Scissors

Embelishments (optional), see step 7

It's probably happened to you before: You reach into your jewelry box to grab your favorite necklace and come up with a tangled clump of necklaces and bracelets. This jewelry stand solves the problem of knotted bangles by hanging them neatly along a display rod. Plus, with this jewelry stand, you can show off your gorgeous duct tape jewelry.

1 Insert the bottle cap or other disk into the end of the cardboard toilet paper tube. If the disc is slightly smaller than the toilet paper tube's opening, simply wrap some tape around the edges of the disk to make it fit.

2 Apply a line of hot glue to the inside of the end of the toilet paper tube and insert the disk.

3 After the glue between the toilet paper tube and the disk has cooled, apply more glue to the face of the disk and glue it to the center of the compact disc. If you don't have a compact disc, you can use a plastic lid. This will be the jewelry stand's base.

4 After the glue has cooled, stand the base upright and place the paper towel tube across the top of the end of the toilet paper tube to form a T shape. Rip off a strip of duct tape and stick it to one side of the toilet paper tube, then wrap it over the paper towel tube and down the other side of the toilet paper tube to secure the two tubes together.

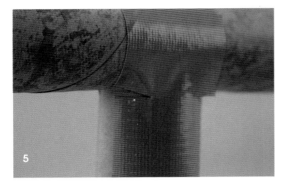

5 Use the scissors to cut little slits near the joint between the two tubes, and smooth the tape down flat.

6 Take a thin strip of duct tape and wrap it around the paper towel tube at the joint of the two tubes, down and around the toilet paper tube at the joint of the two tubes, and back up and around the paper towel tube. This will form a duct tape X across the paper towel tube. Secure the ends of the thin strip by wrapping them around the toilet paper tube.

7 Cover the entire stand in duct tape in the pattern or color of your choice and embellish as you like.

TIP!

KEEP IT STUCK

For extra security, add a little dot of hot glue to the edges of the toilet paper tube before placing the paper towel tube on top of it.

Earring Tree

LEVEL: ●●○○○ ┊ TIME: 35 to 40 minutes

MATERIALS

Toilet paper tube

Duct tape

A large, flat lid with a lip

Approximately 8-by-10-inch piece of thin cardboard (like from a cereal box)

Dry-erase marker

Hole punch

Scissors

Keep your dangly earrings organized with this earring tree. Put all your earrings on the tree to keep them in plain sight, or add just a few for a more decorative look. You can also combine this design with the Jewelry Stand (page 224) to make the ultimate jewelry display.

1 Cover the outside of the toilet paper tube with duct tape, folding the ends of the tape down inside the tube to cover the edges of the tube.

2 Place the lid on the work surface with the lip facing up. Place the toilet paper tube in the center of the lid and tape it to the lid with five to six 1-inch strips of duct tape.

3 Cover the rest of the lid with duct tape.

4 Next, cover both sides of the piece of cardboard with duct tape. Draw a tree shape on the cardboard and cut it out.

5 Use the hole punch to make holes all around the outside of the tree and as far in as the hole punch will reach.

6 Cut two 2-inch slits directly across from one another in the top edge of the toilet paper tube. Slip the tree piece into the two slits. Wrap a piece of duct tape the same color as the tree piece around the top of the toilet paper tube trunk.

7 Hang your earrings from the holes in the tree and the top of the toilet paper tube trunk. Use the lower part of the lid to hold small jewelry items.

A HANGING HOLDER

You can also make a simple hanging earring holder. Just cover the piece of cardboard with duct tape, punch some holes in it, and add hangers like the ones you made for the Dry-Erase Board (page 212).

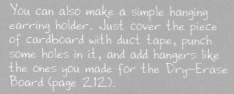

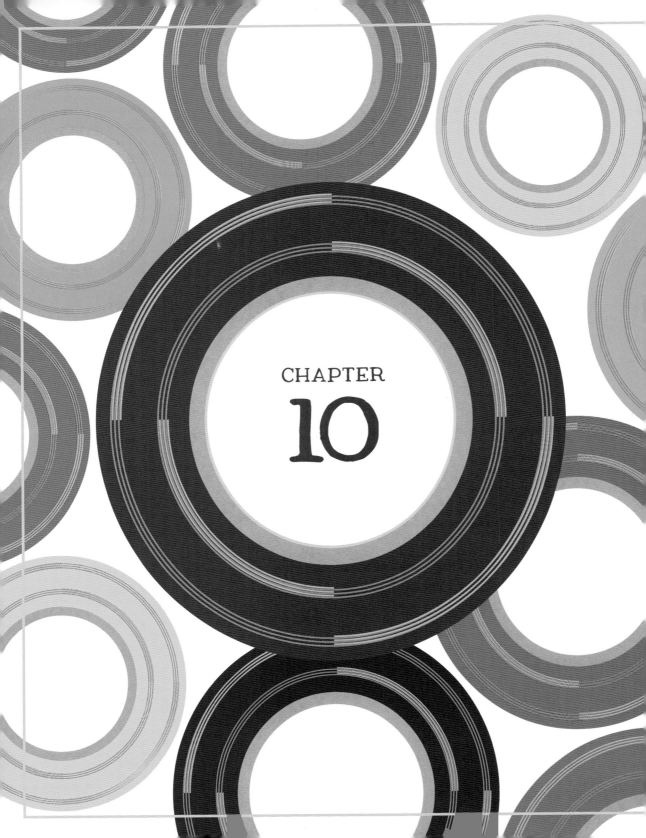

CHAPTER

10

EVERY LAST BIT
OF THE ROLL

In the previous chapters you learned how to use duct tape in almost every way possible—rolling, sticking, ripping, and folding your way to amazing duct tape creations. So what do you do when you get to the end of your roll? Why, make more stuff, of course! Chapter 10 contains quick, simple projects that use duct tape remnants, the last bit of tape on the roll, and even your duct tape roll's cardboard center. Use the techniques in these projects to inspire even more ways to use up every last bit of the duct tape roll.

One of the best things about duct tape is that you can use every bit of it—from the very last cardboard-backed foot of tape to the center of the roll itself.

When you're working on a project and have some leftover pieces of duct tape, stick them on a sheet of parchment paper to save them for later. Even the smallest bits of duct tape can come in handy for embellishments, jewelry, and more. Also, save the end tape from the duct tape rolls—that's the foot or so of tape that is stuck to the cardboard center of the roll. The cardboard backing makes it easy to use for embellishments or other simple projects.

Using the End Tape
End-of-the-Roll Embellishments
Use a patterned hole punch or scissors to make tiny embellishment pieces out of the end-tape pieces. You can stack and layer these patterned pieces to adorn everything from flip-flops to backpacks.

End-Tape Pocket
When you're using a piece of end tape, there's no need to fold the tape over or seal the back to make a pocket, because it's already sealed. Simply add a ¹/₂-inch strip of duct tape around the edges that you need to seal, place your pocket where you want it, and secure with the tape. This is an easy way to make pockets for wallets.

Tassel

End-tape strips are the perfect length for making easy tassels. Just snip the strip every $1/8$ inch and roll it up. Secure the end with a bit of tape.

Tiny Notebook

Cut some scrap paper the size of the piece of end tape. Lay the sheets of paper down on the piece of end tape, fold in the middle, open them up, and staple the creased fold through the sheets of paper and the tape.

Weaving Strips

Save up a lot of end-tape pieces and use them for weaving. Use them just like you would use fold-over strips to make woven duct tape fabric.

Bookmark

A piece of end tape doesn't need much work to become a bookmark. Just trim it to the size of your book and add all the stickers, tassels, and other embellishments you like.

Using the Center of the Roll

Drink Cozy

Glue two cardboard centers together and seal the end with a circle of cardboard, attached either with duct tape or hot glue. Use this cup to hold a soda can, or use it as a dice shaker.

Bangle Bracelet

Glue or tape a piece of yarn to the inside of the cardboard center. Wrap the yarn around the cardboard center until it is completely covered. Secure the end of the yarn inside the cardboard center to make a fun, fuzzy, fanciful bangle.

Mini Shelf

Cut a square of cardboard and attach looped hook holders to the back (see steps 6 and 7 on page 214). Glue cardboard centers to the backing piece in a line to make a cute little shelf for knickknacks.

Carnival Game

Place as many cardboard centers as will fit inside a box and secure them to the bottom of the box with hot glue. Toss balls into the box, trying either to get three in a row or land in a certain pattern inside the cardboard centers.

CONCLUSION

Now that you've honed your duct tape skills on the projects in this book, you might be asking yourself, "What do I do now?" The simple answer is: Anything you want!

You can use the techniques and skills you've learned in *Sticky Fingers* to create pretty much anything you can imagine out of duct tape. Ask yourself what it is you want to make, think about the elements that make up that item, and use the folding, ripping, cutting, and sticking techniques you've learned in this book to make that idea a reality.

You can also add your own flair to any of the projects in this book, making them again and again in different ways. Do you love your duct tape messenger bag? You can make one for a friend, but this time with a braided strap. Try a different kind of closure method every time you make a new duct tape wallet. Cover your next tablet case in rosettes or layered duct tape stickers. The possibilities are endless!

The duct tape world is now open for you to explore. It's up to you where you want to begin, and where you end up.

TEMPLATES

WATERMELON PURSE (page 106)

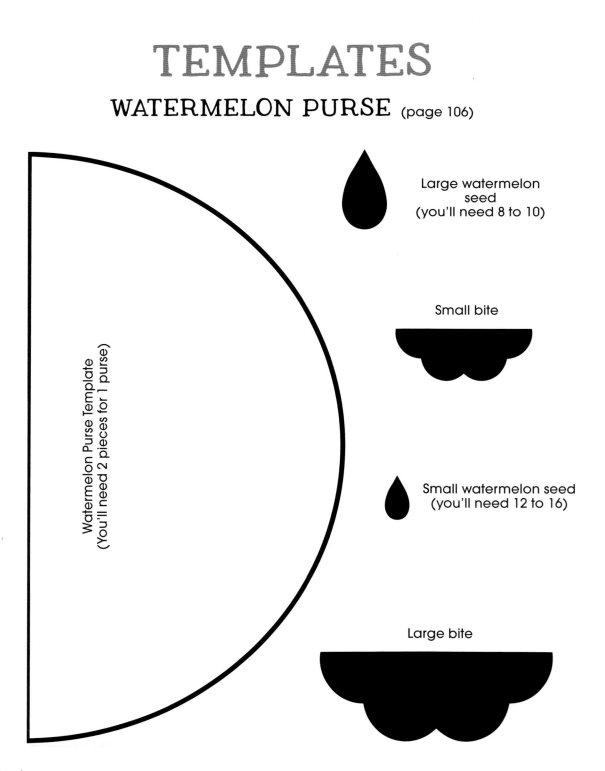

Large watermelon seed
(you'll need 8 to 10)

Small bite

Watermelon Purse Template
(You'll need 2 pieces for 1 purse)

Small watermelon seed
(you'll need 12 to 16)

Large bite

CUPCAKE PURSE (page 110)

Print or trace 2 copies
Tape together at the straight edge

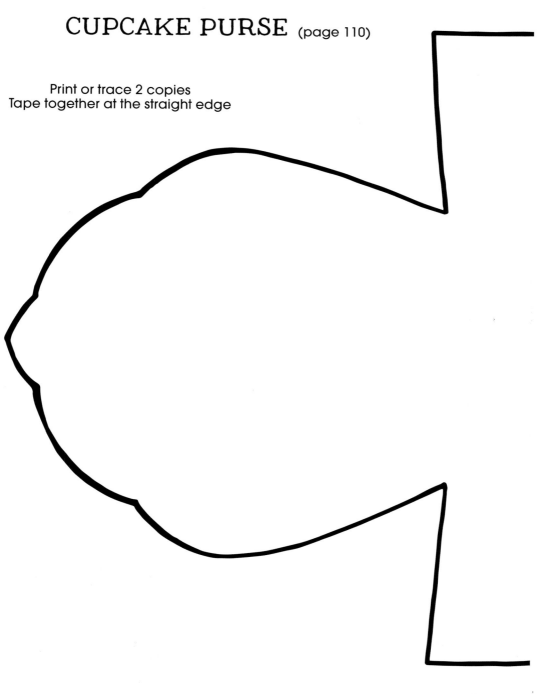

INDEX

accessories. *See also* school
   supplies; wearable items
      makeup case, 114–115
      money keepers, 122–125
      sunglasses case, 116–118
adornments, 21. *See also* flowers
      gift bows, 55–57
      ruffles, 78–79
      stickers, 74–77
      tassels, 50–51, 182–183, 233

bags
      backpacks, 204–207
      beach, checkerboard,
         119–121
      luggage tags for, 184–186
      lunch, 201–203
      messenger, 134–137
      purses, 106–109, 110–113,
         236, 237
      straps for, super-strong, 136
baskets, woven, 218–219
beads, 148–149, 150–151
belts, 178–179
boards, dry-erase, 212–214
book covers, 198–200
bookmarks, 182–183, 233
bows
      basic, 52–54, 157
      fan-fold, 58–59
      gift, 55–57
      for rings, 157
bowties, 52–54, 58–59
bracelets, 150–151, 160–169, 234
button closures, 42–43

carnations, 66–69
cases
      makeup, 114–115
      pencil, 190–192

smartphone, 126–129
sunglasses, 116–118
tablet, 130–133
checkbook keepers, 101–103
checkerboard
      beach bags, 119–121
      game, 215–217
chokers, 170–173
closures
      belt, 179
      button, 42–43
      magnet, 38
      pen, for checkbook, 101–103
      tongue and wraparound,
         39–41
      velcro, 47
      ziploc, 44–45
      zipper, 46
clutch wallets, 86–89, 94–97
cozy, drink, 234
credit card holder, 91
cupcake purse, 110–113, 237

desk organizers, 210–211
dry-erase boards, 212–214
duct tape
      alternatives, 14–15
      brands, 13–14
      center of roll, 234
      end of, 232–233
      fabric, 27–33
      scraps, 153, 168–169, 232–234
      strips, 24–26, 232–233

earring trees, 227–229
end-tape strips, 232–233

fabric, 27–29
      connecting, 97
      felt-backed, 31

for messenger bag, 137
      pouches made from, 35–37
      tarp-backed, 30
      woven, 32–33
felt-backed fabric, 31
first-aid kit, 196–197
flaps, 36–37, 78–79
flowers
      carnations, 66–69
      layered, 64–65, 152–154
      leaf of, 73
      rose petal, 70–72
      rose rings, spike-, 158–159
      rosettes, 60–63
folders, 193–195
frames, picture, 220–223

games, 215–217, 234
gift bows, 55–57

handles, 219
headbands, 146–148

ID holders
      lanyard, 142–144
      wallet, 92, 98–100

jewelry
      beads, 148–149, 150–151
      bracelets, 150–151, 160–169,
         234
      chokers, 170–173
      earring trees, 227–229
      organizing, 224–229
      pendants, 152–154
      rings, 154–159
      stands, 224–226

lanyards, 142–144
leaf, flower stem, 73

locker organizers, 187–189
luggage tags, 184–186
lunch bags, 201–203

magnets
    for closures, 38
    for dry-erase boards, 214
makeup cases, 114–115
mats, self healing cutting, 12
messenger bags, 134–137
money keepers, 122–125. *See also* wallets

necklaces, 152–154, 170–173
notebooks, 233

organization
desk, 210–211
jewelry, 224–229
locker, 187–189
room, 210–211, 218–219, 234
workstation, 18–19

packing tape, 14, 34
pencil cases, 190–192
pendants, layered flower, 152–154
pens
    for checkbook closure, 101–103
    toppers for, 66–69, 70–73
phone cases, 126–129
picture frames, 220–223
pins, 52–54, 140–141
pocket folders, school, 193–195
pocket wallets
    end-tape for, 232
    multi-, 90–93
    trifold, 98–100
    two-, 82–84
pouches, 35–37, 85, 217
purses
    cupcake, 110–113, 237
    watermelon, 106–109, 236

rings, 154–159
room
    baskets, woven, for, 218–219
    checkerboard game for, 215–217
    desk organizers for, 210–211
    dry-erase boards for, 212–214
    jewelry stands in, 224–226
    picture frames for, 220–223
    shelves, mini, for, 234
roses. *See* flowers
ruffles, 78–79

school supplies
    backpacks, 204–207
    book covers, 198–200
    bookmarks, 182–183, 233
    first-aid kit, Altoid tin, 196–197
    folders, pocket, 193–195
    ID, 142–144
    locker organizers, 187–189
    luggage tags, 184–186
    lunch bags, 201–203
    pen toppers, 66–69, 70–73
    pencil cases, 190–192
    supplies, 182–207
scraps, 153, 168–169, 232–234
shelves, mini, 234
smartphone cases, 126–129
spikes, 158–167
stands, jewelry, 224–226
stickers, 74–77
sticky strips, 26
storage, 19, 218–219
strips
    end-tape, 232–233
    fold-over, 24–25
    sticky, 26
    tips, 33, 92, 156
sunglasses case, 116–118
supplies, 12, 18–21. *See also* school supplies

tablet cases, 130–133
tarp-backed fabric, 30
tassels, 50–51, 182–183, 233
technology
    smartphone cases, 126–129
    tablet cases, 130–133
templates, purse, 236–237
3-D pouches, 37
ties, neck, 174–177
tongue closures, 39–41
travel
    luggage tags for, 184–186
    money keepers for, 122–125

velcro closures, 47

wallets
    checkbook keepers, 101–103
    clutch, 86–89, 94–97
    multipocket, 90–93
    pouch, basic, 85
    trifold, 98–100
    two-pocket, 82–84
watermelon purse, 106–109, 236
wearable items. *See also* jewelry
    belts, 178–179
    bowties, 52–54, 58–59
    neck ties, 174–177
    pins, 52–54, 140–141
windows, 34, 92
work surface, 12–13
workstations, 18–19
woven fabric, 32–33, 233
    baskets, 218–219
    for checkerboard beach bag, 119–121

ziploc closures, 44–45
zipper closures, 46

ABOUT THE AUTHOR

Sophie Maletsky grew up surrounded by artists, teachers, playwrights, actors, and storytellers. A self proclaimed "jack of all trades," she began dabbling in puppetry, singing, dancing, acting, clowning, writing, painting, building, designing, and playing the guitar by the ripe old age of thirteen. After earning a degree in Acting, Sophie performed Off-Broadway, in film, and on television before finding her true calling as a children's event planner. For the past twenty years Sophie has been making use of all of those talents to create unique parties for both children and adults.

Sophie is a Nickelodeon Parent's Pick award winner, a certified teacher on curious.com, and a duct tape expert. Sophie's World (sophie-world.com) was launched in 2012 and contains thousands of ideas, how-to's, and videos for crafts, games, and activities.

Sophie lives and creates in San Francisco, California.